Workshop on Language Technology for Digital Historical Archives – with a Special Focus on Central-, (South-) Eastern Europe, Middle East and North Africa (LT-DHA 2019)

Held in Conjunction with the 12th International Conference on Recent Advances in Natural Language Processing

Varna, Bulgaria
9 September 2019

ISBN: 978-1-7138-0298-3

Printed from e-media with permission by:

Curran Associates, Inc.
57 Morehouse Lane
Red Hook, NY 12571

Some format issues inherent in the e-media version may also appear in this print version.

Printed with permission by Curran Associates, Inc. (2020)

Association for Computational Linguistics
209 N. Eighth Street
Stroudsburg, Pennsylvania 18360

Phone: 1-570-476-8006
Fax: 1-570-476-0860

acl@aclweb.org

Additional copies of this publication are available from:

Curran Associates, Inc.
57 Morehouse Lane
Red Hook, NY 12571 USA
Phone: 845-758-0400
Fax: 845-758-2633
Email: curran@proceedings.com
Web: www.proceedings.com

LT-DHA 2019

Proceedings of the Workshop on Language Technology for Digital Historical Archives - with a Special Focus on Central-, (South-)Eastern Europe, Middle East and North Africa

in conjunction with

The 12th International Conference on Recent Advances in Natural Language Processing (RANLP 2019)

5 September, 2019
Varna, Bulgaria

LANGUAGE TECHNOLOGY FOR DIGITAL HISTORICAL ARCHIVES
IN CONJUNCTION WITH THE INTERNATIONAL CONFERENCE
RECENT ADVANCES IN
NATURAL LANGUAGE PROCESSING'2019

PROCEEDINGS

Varna, Bulgaria
5 September 2019

Designed and Printed by INCOMA Ltd.
Shoumen, BULGARIA

Foreword

During the last decades Digital Humanities evolved dramatically, from simple database applications to complex systems involving most recent state-of-the art in Computer Science. Especially Language Technology plays a major role either for processing the metadata of recorded objects or for analyzing and interpreting content. Applying Language Technology methods to objects from humanities in general and historical archives in particular, is a challenge for NLP-related research: data is heterogeneous (image /text), often incomplete (e.g. OCR errors), multilingual within one document (historic documents with Latin or/and classical Greek paragraphs) and difficult to structure (paragraphs, titles, pages are somewhat different in historical texts).
Corpus-based methods, nowadays standard in NLP research, often cannot be applied as the necessary large training data is missing.
Moreover, requirements for tools in Digital Humanities, especially tools dedicated to cultural heritage objects, are different from the ones applied to modern texts. Thus, performing research in Digital Humanities involves also: adapting existent NLP tools to the historical variants of languages; developing tools for new languages; making tools robust to syntactic deviation; and adapting semantic resources. Central and Eastern Europe as well as the Middle East and North Africa were always characterized by a high concentration of languages and cultures, interacting with each other. On a relatively small area texts written with at least 10 alphabets (Arabic, Hebrew, Armenian, Georgian, Greek, Cyrillic, Geez, Syriac and Latin, Coptic) can be found. On the other hand, information within these texts is important beyond the borders of a given language or script. (e.g. often documents in Ge'ez are translations of lost Coptic or ancient Greek texts). Places, Persons, Events have language-dependent denominations but refer to the same individual or geographical location.
Unfortunately, especially in this area many historical documents are in bad condition; many languages or dialects became extinct over the time and their written evidence is rare. Digital methods seem the perfect means for preservation and investigation of this rich cultural heritage asset. However, up to now, concentrated activities seem to be absent, probably also due to the lack of adequate NLP resources and tools. Thus, it is very necessary to evaluate existent technology, monitor current activities, network research teams in this area - all aims of this workshop.
This is the second edition of Language technology for Digital Humanities in Central and (South-)Eastern Europe workshop, held in 2017 at RANLP. In the 2019 International Year of Indigenous Languages this edition expands also to Middle East and North Africa.

The Organisers thank the members of the Programme Committee for the valuable help in selecting the papers.

Cristina Vertan, Petya Osenova and Dimitar Iliev

Organizers:

Cristina Vertan, University of Hamburg
Petya Osenova, Bulgarian cdemy of Sciences and St. Kliment Ohridski University of Sofia
Dimitar Iliev, St. Kliment Ohridski University of Sofia

Program Committee:

Martha Yifiru Abate, University of Addis Ababa
Gabriel Bodard, Institute of Classical Studies, SAS, London
Elie Damaoui, University of Balamand
Antske Fokkens Vrije Universiteit, Amsterdam
Walther v. Hahn, University of Hamburg
Vladislav Kubon, Charles University, Prague
Preslav Nakov, Qatar University
Maciej Ogrodniczuk, Polish Academy of Science
Gabor Proszeky , Catholic University, Budapest
Kiril Simov, Bulgarian Academy of Sciences
Stefan Trausan, Politechnics University, Bucharest
Valeria Vitale, Institute of Classical Studies, SAS, London

Invited Speaker:

Alicia Gonzalez Martinez, University of Hamburg

Table of Contents

Conference Program

09:30–09:40 ***Opening***

09:40–10:30 *Graphemic ambiguous queries on Arabic-scripted historical corpora*
Alicia González Martínez

10:30–11:00 ***Coffee Break***

11:00–12:30 **Corpus Annotation**

11:00–11:30 *Word Clustering for Historical Newspapers Analysis*
Lidia Pivovarova, Elaine Zosa and Jani Marjanen

11:30–12:00 *Geotagging a Diachronic Corpus of Alpine Texts: Comparing Distinct Approaches to Toponym Recognition*
Tannon Kew, Anastassia Shaitarova, Isabel Meraner, Janis Goldzycher, Simon Clematide and Martin Volk

12:00–12:30 *Controlled Semi-automatic Annotation of Classical Ethiopic*
Cristina Vertan

12:30–14:00 ***Lunch***

14:00–16:00 **Integration of NLP and Knowledge Representation**

14:00–14:30 *Implementing an archival, multilingual and Semantic Web-compliant taxonomy by means of SKOS (Simple Knowledge Organization System)*
Francesco Gelati

14:30–15:00 *EU 4 U: An educational platform for the cultural heritage of the EU*
Maria Stambolieva

15:00–15:30 *Modelling linguistic vagueness and uncertainty in historical texts*
Cristina Vertan

15:30–16:00 ***Discussions; Concluding Remarks***

Graphemic ambiguous queries on Arabic-scripted historical corpora

Alicia González Martínez
Hamburg University
Edmund-Siemers-Allee 1, 20146 Hamburg
alicia.gonzalez@uni-hamburg.de

Abstract

Arabic script is a multi-layered orthographic system that consists of a base of archigraphemes, roughly equivalent to the traditional so-called *rasm*, with several layers of diacritics. The archigrapheme represents the smallest logical unit of Arabic script; it consists of the shared features between two or more graphemes, i.e., eliminating diacritics. Archigraphemes are to orthography what archiphonemes are to phonology. An archiphoneme is the abstract representation of two or more phonemes without their distinctive phonological features. For example, in Spanish, occlusive consonants loose their distinctive feature of sonority in syllabic coda position; the words *adjetivo* 'adjective' [aDxe'ti̞βo] and *atleta* 'athlete' [aD'leta] both shared an archiphoneme [D] (in careful speech) in their first syllable, corresponding to the phonemes /d/ and /t/ respectively. In some cases, the neutralisation of two phonemes may cause two words to be homophones. For example, *vid* 'vine' and *bit* 'bit' are both pronounced as [biD]. In paleo-orthographic Arabic script, consonant diacritics were not written down in all positions as it happens in modern Arabic script, where they are mandatory. Consequently, homographic letter blocks were quite common. An additional characteristic of early Arabic script is that graphemic or logical spaces between words did not exist: Arabic orthography preserved the ancient practice of scriptio continua, in which script tries to represent connected speech. Diacritics are signs placed in relation with the archigraphemic skeleton. From a functional point of view, there are two basic types of diacritics: a layer of consonant diacritics for differentiating graphemes and a second layer for vowels. In early script, diacritics are marked in a different colour from the one of the skeleton. Strokes were used for consonant diacritics, whereas dots were used for indicating vowels. In modern Arabic script, dots are instead used for consonant diacritics and they are mandatory. On the other hand, vowels are marked by different types of symbols and are usually optional. Unicode, the standard for digital encoding of language information, evolved from a typographic approach to language and its main concern is modern script. Typography is a technique to reproduce written language based on surface shape. As a consequence, it represents an obstacle for dealing with script from a linguistic point of view, since the same logical grapheme may be rendered using different glyphs. The main problems that arise are the following: 1. Only contemporary everyday use is covered, and that with a typographical approach: Unicode encodes multiple Arabic letters (archigraphemes + consonant diacritics) as single printing units. 2. Some calligraphic variants for the same letter were allowed to have separate Unicode characters. In practice, this means that a search for an Arabic word may yield nothing when typed in a Persian or an Urdu keyboard. This is also why you may find only a fraction of all the results when searching in an Arabic text. 3. There are currently no specialised tools that allow scholars to perform searches on Arabic

Proceedings of the Workshop on Language Technology for Digital Historical Archives in conjuction with RANLP-2019, pages 1–2,
Varna, Bulgaria, Sep 5, 2019.
http://doi.org/10.26615/978-954-452-059-5_001

historical orthography: archigraphemes. Additionally, in order to study early documents written in Arabic script, we need to have search tools that can handle continuous archigraphemic representation, i.e., Arabic script as a scripto continua. In collaboration with Thomas Milo from the Dutch company DecoType, we have developed a search utility that disambiguates and normalises Arabic text in real time and also allows the user to perform archigraphemic search on any Arabic-scripted text. The system is called Yakabikaj (traditional invocation protecting texts against bugs), and show the new perspectives it opens for research in the field of historical digital humanities for Arabic-scripted texts.

Word Clustering for Historical Newspapers Analysis

Lidia Pivovarova **Jani Marjanen** **Elaine Zosa**
University of Helsinki
firstname.lastname@helsinki.fi

Abstract

This paper is a part of a collaboration between computer scientists and historians aimed at development of novel methods for historical newspapers analysis. We present a case study of ideological terms ending with *-ism* suffix in nineteenth-century Finnish newspapers. We propose a two-step procedure to trace differences in word usages over time: training of diachronic embeddings on several time slices and when clustering embeddings of selected words together with their neighbours to obtain historical context. The obtained clusters turn out to be useful for historical studies. The paper also discusses specific difficulties related to development of historian-oriented tools.

1 Introduction

Big corpora of historical newspapers are now digitalized and available for automatic processing. Newspapers have for long been important sources of information for historians and social scientists but massive digitalization opens the possibility to use advanced statistical and NLP methods for historical newspapers. Even though news as a genre have been well-studied in NLP community, switching to historical news imposes additional difficulties for text processing. Automatically digitalized news archives contain much noise related to non-perfect OCR and article separation, as well as less standardised writing practices. Many NLP tools, such as POS-taggers and lemmatizers, are optimized to process modern texts and work less well on historical data. At the same time, historical news share most of the properties of the modern news data: they are biased, incomplete, controversial and apt to change over time.

If historical news are challenging for linguistic analysis, they are even harder for historical studies, since research questions historians are trying to answer are complex and lie far beyond fact discovery. Often they are interested in attitudes, stances, viewpoints, and discourse change in general. These tasks require development of novel methods and instruments that would be oriented specifically at historical research.

We present NewsEye—a research project aimed at development of novel tools and methods for analysis of historical newspapers[1]. The project is a collaboration between digital humanists and computer scientists funded by the European Union's Horizon 2020 research and innovation programme.

This paper focuses on a case study of ideological terms ending with *-ism* suffix—such as *liberalism*, *socialism*, or *conservatism*—in nineteenth century newspapers from Finland. These terms, known as isms, are condensed representations of complex notions that played an important role in political discourse in the nineteenth century (and long after that). Rhetorical usage of isms in historical text has been studied before (Kurunmäki and Marjanen, 2018b,a; Marjanen, 2018), though as far as we are aware this is the first attempt to apply statistical analysis to trace development of these terms in a diachronic newspaper archive.

Not all words ending with *-ism* are ideological. This suffix could be also used for medical terms and diseases (*rheumatism*), scientific terms (*magnetism*), personal traits (*cynicism*), artistic movements (*cubism*), religions (*baptism*) or political practices related to particular persons (*bonapartism*). It is not always possible to draw a strict line between ideologies and other categories.

[1] https://www.newseye.eu/

Proceedings of the Workshop on Language Technology for Digital Historical Archives in conjuction with RANLP-2019, pages 3–10,
Varna, Bulgaria, Sep 5, 2019.
http://doi.org/10.26615/978-954-452-059-5_002

Moreover, the ideological load of these terms might change over time.

We apply a corpus-based analysis to find out how the vocabulary of isms changed in nineteenth century Finnish newspapers and how usage of ideological isms is different from other words with *-ism* suffix. We try to implement a robust analysis procedure that would be applicable to other tasks with minimal human intervention. Our method consists of two main steps: first, we extract from the corpus *all* words with suffix *-ism*, second, we cluster these words and their semantic neighbours in an unsupervised fashion. This procedure does not require a human intervention other than interpretation of results and, consequently, is potentially applicable to other research questions.

2 Data

2.1 Corpora

Newspapers in Finland were published in two main languages—Finnish and Swedish. In the beginning of the nineteenth century the majority of newspapers were published in Swedish, though by the 1880s the Finnish and Swedish newspapers were printed in almost equal amount. The Finnish- and Swedish-language press had a different distribution of topics and exposed slightly different political outlook, though contemporaries often relied on newspapers in both languages (Engman, 2016). Another peculiarity of these data is a censorship accomplished by the Russian Empire government. The censorship was abandoned in 1905, which led to an outburst of socialistic rhetoric in the press, especially in the Finnish-language newspapers since they were more likely to have a rural or working-class background.

We use a digitalized collection of nineteenth-century Finnish newspapers freely available from the National Library of Finland (Pääkkönen et al., 2016). We use the full Swedish and Finnish data from 1820 to 1917, treating them as two separate corpora. Each corpus is split into five double-decades. The total amount of words in both corpora is presented in Table 1.

In Figure 1 we present relative frequencies for the selection of most frequent isms in our data. It can be seen that a proportion of isms are growing over time. The plots demonstrate some difference between the datasets: e.g. *patriotism* is much more frequent in the Swedish dataset.

Time slice	Millions of words	
	FINNISH	SWEDISH
1820-1839	1.3	25.5
1840-1859	10.3	77.9
1860-1879	90.6	326.7
1880-1899	805.3	966.9
1900-1917	2439.0	953.0
Total	3346.6	2355.2

Table 1: Corpus size by double decade.

Both corpora are lowercased and lemmatized using LAS, an open-source language-analysis tool (Mäkelä, 2016).[2] LAS is a meta-analysis tool that provides a wrapper for many existing tools developed for specific tasks and languages. Though LAS supports multiple languages, most efforts were done to process Finnish data, including historical Finnish. The output for our Swedish data is more noisy. In particular, the Swedish LAS lemmatizer is unable to predict lemma for out-of-vocabulary words, e.g. *boulangismen* (definite form of 'boulangism'). Thus we applied the additional normalization and convert all words ending with *-ismen* or *-ismens* into *-ism* forms. For all other words we use the LAS output; implementation of proper Swedish lemmatization is beyond the scope of this paper.

3 Approach

3.1 Diachronic embeddings

We train continuous embeddings (Mikolov et al., 2013) on each double-decade. We use Gensim Word2Vec implementation (Řehůřek and Sojka, 2010) using the Skip-gram model, with a vector dimensionality of 100, window size of 5 and a frequency threshold of 100—only lemmas that appear more than 100 times within a double decade are used for training. One hundred is an arbitrary and rather conservative threshold that ensures that each word in a model has reliable amount of context and embeddings are trustworthy. On the other hand, we lose some *isms* because they appear less than 100 times in a double-decade. For instance, *patriotism* and *liberalism* appear for the first time in the Swedish corpus in 1791 and 1820 respectively, but the corresponding vectors exist in our models starting from 1820-1839 and 1840-1859 respectively. The number of distinct isms in our models is presented in Table 2.

[2] `https://github.com/jiemakel/las`

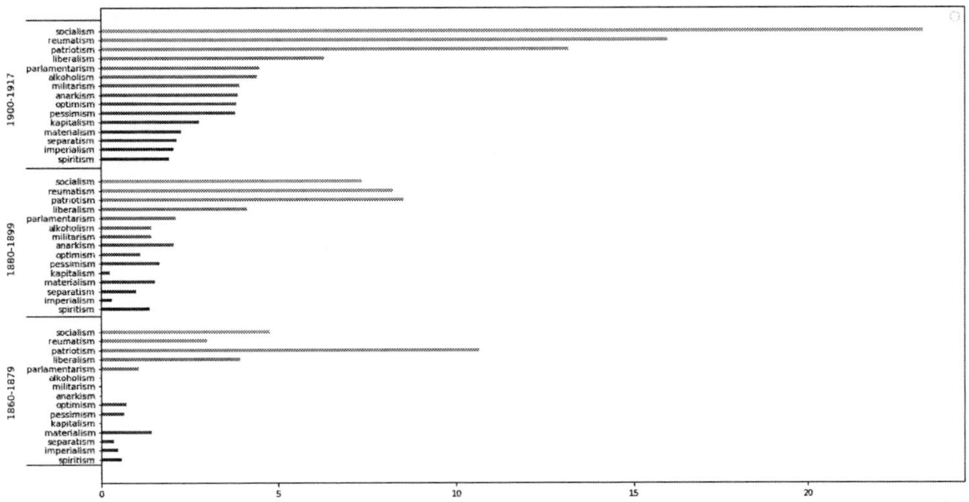

(a) SWEDISH

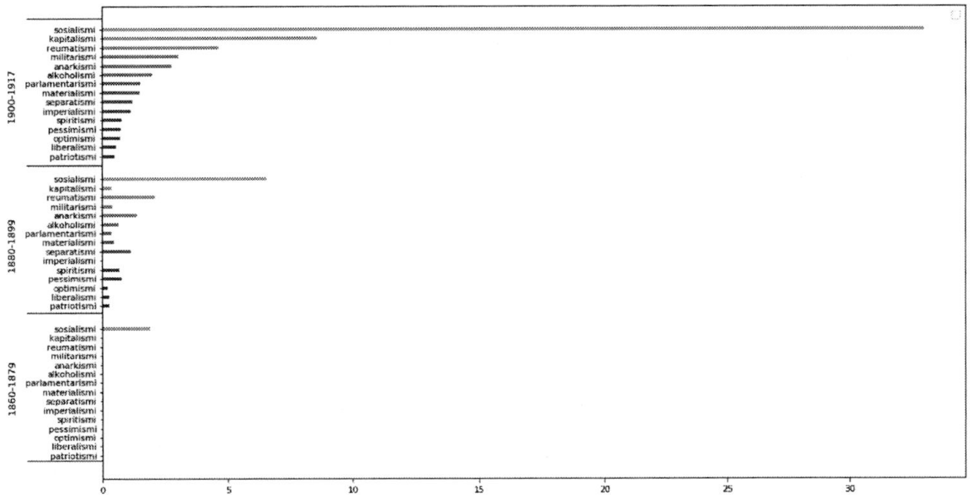

(b) FINNISH

Figure 1: A selection of the most frequent words ending with suffix *-ism*/*ismi*. The x-axis presents relative frequency in items per million.

Since training word embeddings is a stochastic process, the particular values of vectors do not stay close across runs, though distances between words are quite stable. To ensure that embeddings are stable across time slices, we follow the approach proposed in (Kim et al., 2014): embeddings for $t + 1$ time slice are initialized with vectors built on t; then training continues using new data. The learning rate value is set to the end learning rate of the previous model, to prevent models from diverging rapidly. This approach has been previously used in (Hengchen et al., 2019) with slightly different data.

3.2 Clustering

We cluster word embeddings into semantically close groups using Affinity Propagation clustering technique (Frey and Dueck, 2007). The main advantages of Affinity Propagation are that it detects number of clusters automatically and is able to produce clusters of various sizes.

FINNISH				
Time slice	*ism*	*close*	*cluster*	*select*
1820 - 1839	0	-	-	-
1840 - 1859	0	-	-	-
1860 - 1879	1	157	1	12
1880 - 1899	35	5977	20	442
1900 - 1917	119	8940	70	1543

SWEDISH				
Time slice	*ism*	*close*	*cluster*	*select*
1820 - 1839	3	724	3	49
1840 - 1859	17	1845	12	211
1860 - 1879	61	5229	31	669
1880 - 1899	120	12233	54	1320
1900 - 1917	137	11858	56	1387

Table 2: Number of distinct words used on various steps of the algorithm: ***ism*** is a number of distinct words with suffix *-ism*, ***close*** is a number of words, which cosine similarity to at least one ism is higher than 0.5, ***cluster*** is a number of clusters that contain at least one ism, ***select*** is a number of words in these clusters.

Affinity Propagation has been previously used for various language analysis tasks, including collocation clustering into semantically related classes (Kutuzov et al., 2017) and unsupervised word sense induction (Alagić et al., 2018). Both papers pay special attention to fine-tuning of the algorithm and selection of hyper-parameters. We cannot tune the algorithm due to the lack of gold standard, which is typical for exploratory historical research. We use standard implementation from the Scikit-learn package (Pedregosa et al., 2011), with default parameters.

The procedure works as follows. In the data selection step we extract from the corpus all words with a cosine similarity of less than 0.5 to any *ism*. Then we perform clustering on this enriched dataset. Finally, the clusters are filtered so that only clusters that contain at least one *ism* word are presented for the qualitative analysis.

The number of words used on various steps of analysis is presented in Table 2. It can be seen from the table is that the number *isms* in the Finnish data is much smaller than for the Swedish data. In particular in the two double decades there are no Finnish ism above the frequency threshold. That could be partially explained by the smaller amount of Finnish newspapers but also by the difference between languages. The suffix *ismi* is not as productive in the Finnish language and used mostly with loan words, while Swedish more readily adopt *ism* suffix. In many cases Swedish words ending with *-ism* are translated into Finnish using native suffixes. For example, Swedish *katolicism* is translated into Finnish as *katolilaisuus*. In some cases, two words with same meaning but different endings existed in the same time period, e.g. *protestantismi* and *protestanttisuus* or *nationalismi* and *kansallisuusaate*.

It can be seen in the table that though 0.5 is an arbitrary threshold up to 90% of words selected using this threshold are filtered out after the clustering. The number of selected clusters is generally smaller than the number of words with suffix *ism* since isms tend to cluster together.

4 Results and Observations

One of the main difficulties for our work is a lack of gold standard annotations. We cannot know in advance how the words should be clustered, especially the most problematic ideological terms, which are the main objects of our study. However, we can make several common-sense assumptions on the expected outcome. For example, it would be reasonable to expect that disease names should not appear in the same cluster with philosophical concepts or that artistic movements should be clustered together. In this section we present several observations, starting with those that can be considered as "sanity checks" for the clustering.

Rheumatism

In the nineteenth century rheumatism was often mentioned in the medical advertisements. Automatic advertisement filtering in historical news is not a trivial task since advertisements were less regulated, contained more text and looked similar to other articles. Moreover, such filtering is not always necessary since advertisements might provide researchers with valuable insights[3].

We use the entire corpora to build embeddings, and as a consequence *rheumatism* is one of the most frequent words with suffix *-ism* in our data, as can be seen in Figure 1 (for the Swedish data we sum up counts for spelling variants *reumatism* and *rheumatism*).

Table 3, which shows all clusters from our Finnish data that contain words related to rheuma-

[3]See for example a recent blog post analyzing gender stereotypes in the nineteenth century drug advertisements: https://www.newseye.eu/blog/news/british-drug-advertising-in-the-19th-century-through-the-prism-of-gender/

1880-1899	1900-1917
reumatismi 'rheumatism'	*vähäverisyys* 'anaemia' *risatauti* 'lymphadenitis' *veripuute* 'anaemia' *heillou* 'weakness?'$_{ocr}$
luuvalo 'gout'	*nivelreumatismi* 'arthritis' *epämuodostuma* 'deformity' *kohju* 'hernia'
luumalo 'gout'$_{ocr}$	*kroonillinen* 'chronic' *mahatauti* 'gastroenteritis' *mahakatarri* 'gastritis'
iskä '?' *latus* '?'	*suolitauti* 'salt deposits' *riisitauti* 'rickets' *hermovaiva* 'nerve ailment'
liikavarvas 'callus'	*verenvähyys* 'anaemia' *ruumisvika* 'body problem' *veritauti* 'blood disease'
kihti 'gout'	*lihavuus* 'obesity' *kaljupäisyys* 'boldness' *verettömyydä* 'verettömyydä'
säilöstystauti 'canning disease'	*heikkohermoisuus* 'neurasthenia' *lihanen* 'obese' *sukupuoli-* 'sex/gender'$_{ocr}$
jalkahiki 'foot odor'	*sappitauti* 'biliary disease' *heitlous* 'weakness'$_{ocr}$ *selkäydintauti* 'spinal cord disease'
kivuton 'painless'	*hermoheikkous* 'neurasthenia' *ruokasulatushäiriö* 'digestion problem'
reumatillinen 'rheumatic'	*kalvetustauti* 'anaemia' *vinous* 'skewness' *tautitila* 'disease place'
reumaatillinen 'rheumatic'	*vähäverinen* 'anaemic' *epämuodostua* 'to deform' *hermosairaus* 'neuropathy'

1900-1917
reumatismi 'rheumatism' *hiustauti* 'hair disease' *jäsensärky* 'limb ache'
hermo 'nerve' *oxygeno* '?' *vatsakatar* 'gastritis' *umpitauti* 'constipation'
nuha 'rhinitis' *hermotautinen* 'neurotic' *topioli* '?' *kurkkukatarri* 'pharyngitis'
parannuskeino 'remedy' *hoitokeino* 'cure' *spirosiini* 'spirosin' *lazarol* 'lazarol'
lääkitä 'to medicate' *kotilääke* 'home medicine' *reumaattinen* 'rheumatic'
hammastauti 'tooth disease' *rautaliuos* 'iron care' *jäsenkolotus* 'limb ache'
leini 'rheumatism' *linjamentti* 'ointment' *parannusaine* 'betterment' *vilustuminen* 'cold'
luuvalo 'gout' *latsaro* '?' *hengityselimettauti* 'respiratory disease'

Table 3: Clusters containing Finnish words related to rheumatism. Original words are presented in italics together with English translations in quotes. *ocr* means the word is incorrectly spelled due to OCR errors; "?" means "impossible to translate"—these are mostly fragments of words appearing due to OCR errors. Bottom left: an advertisement of a rheumatism medicine from *Hufvudstadsbladet*, 01.03.1912, no. 59, p. 15

tism. It can be seen that *rheumatism* does not interfere with other isms: the clusters entirely consist of words related to drugs, medical procedures, diseases and other physical conditions, such as baldness or obesity. In that sense clusters are rather precise and justify our algorithmic decisions.

On the other hand, cluster may be too fine-grained for our needs. In the 1900-1917 double-decade there are two clusters with similar meaning: one related to *reumatismi* 'rheumatism', another to *nivelreumatismi* '(rheumatoid) arthritis'. Very similar results were obtained on the Swedish data: *reumatism* 'rheumatism' and *ledgngsreumatism* 'arthritis' are split into different clusters even though spelling variants *rheumatism* and *reumatism* are clustered together.

We suggest that the fine-grained clustering does not as such reflect semantic differences, but the differences in distribution come from slightly different uses in the newspapers. While there are similarities it seems that rheumatism appears more often in medical advertising whereas the arthritis seems to be more likely to appear in text content with a more ambitious take on educating the public about medical issues.

Spiritism

In Table 4 we present clusters obtained from Swedish data that contain the word *spiritism*. The cluster for the 1860-1879 double decade contains a few words related to this popular practice such as *pressensé* and *kabal* though most of its content are names of famous scientists and writers. This might be an error: some of the names might be a person that were discussed in the context of spiritism (as objects to spiritism or as scientific authorities), e.g. Aristotle or Galileo, and others are words that are similar to these names. In other words, *spiritism* might be an outlier in this cluster.

It might also be the case that spiritism was sometimes used as 'spiritualism' and Darwin and the others were discussed in this context. This would require a further analysis.

The clusters for the latter double-decades do not expose such problems and consist mostly of words clearly related to spiritism including some very specific terms, such as *transmigration*, and more general esoteric concepts, such *theosophy* or *freemasonry*. The 1880-1899 cluster might also reflect a contemporary discussion on relations between science and mysticism, since it contains such isms as *positivism* or *darwinism*.

Separatism

Separatism is a more tricky concept, which undergo a noticeable usage change in our datasets as can be seen in Table 5, where we present clusters for Swedish *separatism*.

1860-1879	1880-1899	1900-1917
spiritism 'spiritism'	*spiritism* 'spiritism' *teosofi* 'theosophy'	*spiritism* 'spiritism' *hypnotism* 'hypnotism'
pressensé 'presence' (Fr)	*frimureri* 'freemasonry' *feder* '?'	*andevärld* 'spirit world' *teosofisk* 'theosophic'
pater 'pater' *voltaire* 'Voltaire'	*mysterium* 'mystery' *spiritualism* 'spiritualism'	*spiritistisk* 'spiritualistic' *telepati* 'telepathy'
darwin 'Darwin' *renan* 'Renan'	*darwinism* 'darwinism' *positivism* 'positivism'	*själavandring* 'transmigration'
zola 'Zola' *newton* 'Newton'	*buddism* 'Buddhism' *darvinism* 'darvinism'	*trolleri* 'magic' *journalism* 'journalism'
balzac 'Balzac' *michelet* 'Michelet'	*vegetarianism* 'vegetarianism' *astrologi* 'astrology'	*ockult* 'occult' *astrologisk* 'astrological'
galilei 'Galileo' *corneille* 'Corneille'	*teosofisk* 'theosophic' *bibelkritik* 'Bible criticism'	*astrologi* 'astrology' *frimureri* 'freemasonry'
aristoteles 'Aristotle' *kabal* 'cabal'	*metafysik* 'metaphysics' *teosofien* 'theosophy'	*gondiagnos* 'eye diagnosis' *alkemi* 'alchemy'
oppert 'Oppert' *rousseau* 'Rousseau'	*darvin* 'Darvin' *darvins* 'Darvin'	*clairvoyance* 'clairvoyance'(Fr)
proudhon 'Proudhon' *zolas* 'Zola'	*utvecklingslära* 'evolution' *malthus* 'Malthus'	*tankeläsning* 'mind reading'
quand 'when' (Fr) *loyson* 'Loyson'	*själavandring* 'transmigration'	*tungomlstalande* 'tongues'

Table 4: Clusters containing Swedish word *spiritism.*

1860-1879	1880-1899	1900-1917
separatism 'separatism'	*separatism* 'separatism' *rent* '?'	*separatism* 'separatism' *riksid* 'national idea'$_{ocr}$
mysticism 'mysticism' *naturalism* 'naturalism'	*finskhet* 'Finnishness' *fennomanins* 'Fennomania'	*statsid* 'state idea'$_{ocr}$ *rikspolitik* 'national policy'
darwinism 'darwinism' *moral* 'morality'	*fennomani* 'Fennomania' *svenskhet* 'Swedishness'	*bourgeoisins* 'bourgeoisie' *byråkratien* 'bureaucracy'
tidsanda 'zeitgeist' *krass* 'crass' *utopi* 'utopia'	*fennomanin* 'Fennomania' *vikingaparti* 'Viking party'	*samhällsopinion* 'social opinion'
materialistisk 'materialistic' *otro* 'incredible'	*språkpolitik* 'language policy' *publicistisk* 'publishing'	*sträfvandenas* '?' *rikskomplex* 'national complex'
rationalistisk 'rationalistic' *wantro* '?'	*partiagitation* 'party agitation' *partiyra* '?'	*nationalitet-* 'national'$_{ocr}$ *santryska* 'true Russian'
menniskonaturen 'human nature' *tidehvarfvets* '?'	*partifanatism* 'party fanaticism'	*ämbetsmannavälde* 'officialdom'
materialism 'materialism' *materialist* 'materialistic'	*språkgräl* 'language quarrel'	*gränsmärke* 'borderline' *gränsmark* 'borderline'$_{ocr}$
konservatism 'conservatism'	*språkfanatism* 'language fanaticism'	*riksenhet* 'national assembly'
idealism 'idealism' *rationalism* 'rationalism'	*språkfråga* 'language question'	*samhällskraft* 'social force' *statlighet* 'statehood'
negation 'negation' *abstraktion* 'abstraction'	*spräkfrägan* 'language question'	*frihetssträvande* 'freedom-aspiring' *wäldets* '?'
idealistisk 'idealistic'	*ljusskygghet* 'photophobia'	*riksmakt* 'national power' *självhärskarmakten* '?'

Table 5: Swedish clusters containing word *separatism*

1880-1899	1900-1917
separatismi 'separatism' *ruotsi-kiihkoinen* 'Svekoman' *ruotsinmielinen* 'Swedish-minded'	*separatismi* 'separatism'
ruotsalaisuus 'Swedishness' *viikinki* 'Viking' *ruotsi-mielinen* 'Swedish-minded'	*nationalismi* 'nationalism' *natsionalismi* 'nationalism'
fennomaani 'Fennoman' *epäkansallinen* 'anti-national' *viikingit* 'Vikings'	*opportunismi* 'opportunism' *natfionalismi* 'nationalism'$_{ocr}$
separatisti 'separatist' *ruotsikko* 'Swedish'(person) *miikinki* 'Viking'$_{ocr}$ *pöppö* '?'	*eristäytyminen* 'isolation' *kansalliskiihko* 'nationalism'
miikingit 'Vikings'$_{ocr}$ *suomimielinen* 'Finnish-minded' *ruotsi-mielisyys* 'Swedish-mindedness'	*intelligens* 'intelligence' *länsieurooppalainen* 'Western-European'
wiitinki 'Viking'$_{ocr}$ *wiilinki* 'Viking'$_{ocr}$ *miitinki* 'Viking'$_{ocr}$ *ruotsimielinen* 'Swedish-minded'	*rotutaistelu* 'race fight' *vapaamielisyy* 'liberalism'$_{ocr}$
suomi-kiihkoinen 'Fennoman' *fennoman* 'Fennoman' *henkiheimolainen* 'soul mate'	*sanomalehdistö!* 'press' *antipatia* 'antipathy'
dagbladilainen 'member of the Dagblad circle' *miiking* 'Viking'$_{ocr}$ *fennomani* 'Fennoman'	*kansallinenviha* 'national anger' *kiihkokansallisuus* 'nationalism'
wiiking 'Viking'$_{ocr}$ *fennomaaninen* 'Fennoman' *ruotsikiihkoisuus* 'Svekomania'	*eristäytyä* 'self-isolate' *liittolaisuus* 'alliance'
wiilinli 'Viking'$_{ocr}$ *miikinkilehti* 'Vikings' newspaper'$_{ocr}$ *suomenmielinen* 'Finnish-minded'$_{ocr}$	*vihamieli-syy* 'hostility'$_{ocr}$ *kansallinenylpeys* 'national pride'
miikinkiläinen 'Vikingish'$_{ocr}$ *ruolsinmielinen* 'Swedish-minded' *ruotsiliihloinen* 'Svekoman'$_{ocr}$	*kielipolitiikka* 'language policy'
herranenluokka '?' *miikingilehti* 'Vikings' newspaper'$_{ocr}$ *epälansallinen* 'anti-national'$_{ocr}$	*kansallinenliike* 'national movement'

Table 6: Finnish clusters containing word *separatismi*

Most of the words in the 1860-1879 cluster are religious, philosophical or scientific notions, thus we can assume that the cluster presents a religious context of *separatism*. The 1880-1899 cluster contains completely different set of words, including reference to specific political entities, such as Fennomans movement and contains rather emotional expressions, such as *agitation* or *fanaticism*. These words are related to a contemporary discussion about national identity and national language. The 1900-1917 cluster is again different from the previous two and contains more general political lexis. Thus, we can suggest that at the beginning the notion of separatism had mostly religious meaning, when it was adopted by a limited number of liberals and finally spread into a more general political discourse.

The Finnish clusters for *separatismi*, presented in Table 6, are quite similar to Swedish. The main difference is that in the 1860-1879 the word is mentioned less than 100 times and as a consequence excluded from our models. But the 1880-1899 and 1900-1917 Finnish clusters follow the same pattern: the former contains quite specific references, while the latter consists of more general political words.

The change in the distribution of *separatism* seems to be related to a change in the dominant context in which it was discussed (from religious context to a political context). This also entails some degree of semantic change.

This contextual and semantic shift could be to some extent visible from changes in the nearest neighbours of *separatism* presented in Figure 2a. However, nearest neighbours produce a more vague overview: for example, religious isms, such as *pietism*, are presented among nearest neighbours of *separatism* in 1860-1879. Similarly, the overlap between Finnish clusters, shown in Table 6, and nearest neighbours of *separatismi*, presented in Figure 6 is very limited.

(a) SWEDISH

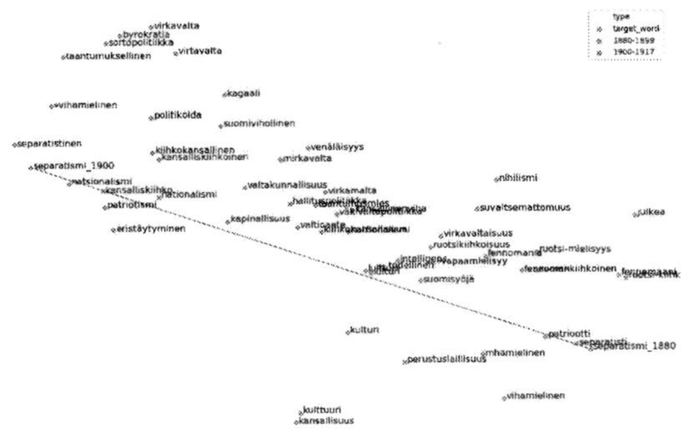

(b) FINNISH

Figure 2: tSNE plot word *separatism* and its nearest neighbours across time slices.

This can be explained by the nature of the clustering procedure: each word can be among the nearest neighbours for any number of other words while Affinity Propagation assign a word to exactly one cluster so that *socialism* and *katolicism* are separated in clusters of their own. The difference between outputs demonstrates an added value of the clustering, which selects only one word split among many possibilities provided by embeddings. At the same time, this also means loss of information, especially for polysemous words.

5 Conclusion and Further Work

We presented our ongoing work aimed at the implementation of tools facilitating historical studies of newspaper archives. We proposed an unsupervised procedure to trace differences in word usage over time. The procedure consists of two major steps: training of diachronic embeddings and then clustering embeddings of selected words together with their neighbours to obtain historical context.

In this paper we applied this procedure to a group of words ending with suffix *-ism*. The method allowed us to distinguish ideological terms, such as *socialism* from other words with the same suffix, such as disease names or scientific terms. This promising result suggests that it is worthy to further elaborate the proposed method.

At this stage of the work we are unable to draw any clear conclusions related to usage of isms in the nineteenth century in Finland. Clusters that contain ideological words are the most problematic for the interpretation, which is not surprising given complex nature of the underlying concepts.

Nevertheless, we consider the obtained clusters useful for historical studies since they provide a researcher with a condensed representation of word usages in a large corpus. This is a novel way to look at historical data, which might be especially useful in combination with other tools such as named entity recognition or topic modelling.

Further improvements of the method should include both parts, namely embeddings and clustering. We plan to try building *continuous* word embeddings (Dubossarsky et al., 2019; Gillani and Levy, 2019; Rosenfeld and Erk, 2018; Yao et al., 2018) that would allow us to investigate gradual semantic shifts rather than split data into discrete time slices. Improvement of clustering might include fine-tuning of the algorithm parameters, though this is quite hard to do without manually annotated data. Thus, our main focus would be in finding other applications for the proposed procedure that would be meaningful from a historical research point of view and easily assessed at the same time.

We will also continue development of complex instruments for historical news analysis that would utilize clustering techniques together with other automatic text analysis methods.

Acknowledgements

We are grateful to Simon Hengchen and Mark Granroth-Wilding for the help with data preparation. This work has been supported by the European Unions Horizon 2020 research and innovation programme under grants 770299 (NewsEye) and 825153 (EMBEDDIA).

References

Domagoj Alagić, Jan Šnajder, and Sebastian Padó. 2018. Leveraging lexical substitutes for unsupervised word sense induction. In *Thirty-Second AAAI Conference on Artificial Intelligence*.

Haim Dubossarsky, Simon Hengchen, Nina Tahmasebi, and Dominik Schlechtweg. 2019. Time-out: Temporal referencing for robust modeling of lexical semantic change. In *The 57th Annual Meeting of the Association for Computational Linguistics (ACL)*.

Max Engman. 2016. *Språkfrågan: Finlandssvenskhetens uppkomst 1812-1922*. Svenska litteratursällskapet i Finland.

Brendan J Frey and Delbert Dueck. 2007. Clustering by passing messages between data points. *science* 315(5814):972–976.

Nabeel Gillani and Roger Levy. 2019. Simple dynamic word embeddings for mapping perceptions in the public sphere. In *NAACL HLT 2019*. page 94.

Simon Hengchen, Ruben Ros, and Jani Marjanen. 2019. A data-driven approach to the changing vocabulary of the nation in English, Dutch, Swedish and Finnish newspapers, 1750-1950. In *In Proceedings of the Digital Humanities (DH) conference 2019, Utrecht, The Netherlands*.

Yoon Kim, Yi-I Chiu, Kentaro Hanaki, Darshan Hegde, and Slav Petrov. 2014. Temporal analysis of language through neural language models. *ACL 2014* page 61.

Jussi Kurunmäki and Jani Marjanen. 2018a. Isms, ideologies and setting the agenda for public debate. *Journal of Political Ideologies* 23(3):256–282. https://doi.org/10.1080/13569317.2018.1502941.

Jussi Kurunmäki and Jani Marjanen. 2018b. A rhetorical view of isms: An introduction. *Journal of Political Ideologies* 23(3):241–255.

Andrey Kutuzov, Elizaveta Kuzmenko, and Lidia Pivovarova. 2017. Clustering of Russian adjective-noun constructions using word embeddings. In *Proceedings of the 6th Workshop on Balto-Slavic Natural Language Processing*. pages 3–13.

Eetu Mäkelä. 2016. LAS: an integrated language analysis tool for multiple languages. *The Journal of Open Source Software* 1.

Jani Marjanen. 2018. Ism concepts in science and politics. *Contributions to the History of Concepts* 13(1).

Tomas Mikolov, Kai Chen, Greg S Corrado, and Jeffrey Dean. 2013. Efficient estimation of word representations in vector space. In *NIPS*.

Tuula Pääkkönen, Jukka Kervinen, Asko Nivala, Kimmo Kettunen, and Eetu Mäkelä. 2016. Exporting Finnish digitized historical newspaper contents for offline use. *D-Lib Magazine* 22(7/8).

F. Pedregosa, G. Varoquaux, A. Gramfort, V. Michel, B. Thirion, O. Grisel, M. Blondel, P. Prettenhofer, R. Weiss, V. Dubourg, J. Vanderplas, A. Passos, D. Cournapeau, M. Brucher, M. Perrot, and E. Duchesnay. 2011. Scikit-learn: Machine learning in Python. *Journal of Machine Learning Research* 12:2825–2830.

Radim Řehůřek and Petr Sojka. 2010. Software framework for topic modelling with large corpora. In *Proceedings of the LREC 2010 Workshop on New Challenges for NLP Frameworks*. ELRA, Valletta, Malta, pages 45–50.

Alex Rosenfeld and Katrin Erk. 2018. Deep neural models of semantic shift. In *Proceedings of the 2018 Conference of the North American Chapter of the Association for Computational Linguistics: Human Language Technologies, Volume 1 (Long Papers)*. pages 474–484.

Zijun Yao, Yifan Sun, Weicong Ding, Nikhil Rao, and Hui Xiong. 2018. Dynamic word embeddings for evolving semantic discovery. In *The 11th ACM International Conference on Web Search and Data Mining*.

Geotagging a Diachronic Corpus of Alpine Texts: Comparing Distinct Approaches to Toponym Recognition

Tannon Kew, Anastassia Shaitarova, Isabel Meraner, Janis Goldzycher
Simon Clematide and Martin Volk

Institute of Computational Linguistics, University of Zurich, Switzerland
{*tannon.kew, anastassia.shaitarova, isabel.meraner, janis.goldzycher*}@*uzh.ch*,
{*simon.clematide, volk*}@*cl.uzh.ch*

Abstract

Geotagging historic and cultural texts provides valuable access to heritage data, enabling location-based searching and new geographically related discoveries. In this paper, we describe two distinct approaches to geotagging a variety of fine-grained toponyms in a diachronic corpus of alpine texts. By applying a traditional gazetteer-based approach, aided by a few simple heuristics, we attain strong high-precision annotations. Using the output of this earlier system, we adopt a state-of-the-art neural approach in order to facilitate the detection of new toponyms on the basis of context. Additionally, we present the results of preliminary experiments on integrating a small amount of crowdsourced annotations to improve overall performance of toponym recognition in our heritage corpus.

1 Introduction

Identifying spatial information in cultural and historical corpora is a crucial step in putting these texts on the map. Geotagging describes the task of establishing the connection between textual mentions of geographic locations, also known as toponyms, with geographic information systems (Amitay et al., 2004; Lieberman et al., 2010). This natural language processing (NLP) task provides the essential information required for location-based search queries (Moncla et al., 2014) and has thus found many uses in diverse fields, such as geography, question answering, bio-medicine and digital humanities, among others.

Geotagging consists of two main tasks. First, toponym mentions must be identified in text. This step, known as toponym recognition, can be seen as a location-oriented subtask of named entity recognition (NER), which is more broadly interested in identifying and classifying textual mentions of various entities such as people, locations and organisations. Second, an identified toponym needs to be linked to its true geographic referent via a unique identifier stored in an external knowledge base. This step, which we refer to as toponym resolution, often requires disambiguating identified toponyms in order to establish that link.[1]

When it comes to handling historical and cultural documents, lexical and orthographic shifts in language as well as political and administrative changes make geotagging, and NER in general, particularly challenging. In this paper, we describe our heritage corpus of alpine and mountaineering texts (Section 2), which poses unique challenges due to its domain and diachronicity. We detail two distinct efforts in geotagging a variety of fine-grained toponyms in this corpus, focusing primarily on German[2]. First, we give an overview of an earlier gazetteer-based approach oriented towards high-precision annotations (Section 3). Then, we present a current state-of-the-art neural approach which takes advantage of recent advances in sequence labelling techniques, the high-precision gazetteer-based output and a small number of

[1]In the relevant literature, both toponym recognition and toponym resolution have many guises which are used somewhat interchangeably (cf. Moncla et al., 2014; Gritta et al., 2018). We follow the naming conventions provided by Leidner (2007) and Lieberman et al. (2010) and adopt the term 'geotagging' to refer to the combined task of toponym recognition and resolution.

[2]Neural experiments involving French are currently underway.

Proceedings of the Workshop on Language Technology for Digital Historical Archives in conjuction with RANLP-2019, pages 11–18,
Varna, Bulgaria, Sep 5, 2019.
http://doi.org/10.26615/978-954-452-059-5_003

crowdsourced annotations (Section 4). Finally, we evaluate and compare these two approaches and provide results from preliminary experiments on our annotation platform which aims to bring humans into the loop for geotagging heritage data (Section 5).

2 A Heritage Corpus of Alpine Texts

Our corpus consists of over 150 years of alpine and mountaineering articles. The majority of the corpus comes from the yearbooks published by the Swiss Alpine Club (SAC) between 1864 and 2015. Also included in the corpus are the articles from the journal of the British Alpine Club from 1969 to 2008. As such, it is a largely multilingual corpus containing texts in German, French, English, Italian and Romansh. Table 1 provides an overview of general corpus statistics for each language. The corpus is rich in geographic references and is a valuable resource detailing many aspects of life in the mountains. Topics covered range from mountaineering and hiking expeditions, flora and fauna, geography, and geological changes to social, cultural and linguistic diversity in alpine regions.

Being a diarchronic heritage corpus, its development has posed a number of challenges regarding digitisation and linguistic annotation. Numerous experiments have been undertaken to semantically enrich this corpus as both a historic and a linguistic resource. These include, but are not limited to, a novel approach to correcting optical character recognition (OCR) errors (Clematide et al., 2016); gazetteer and rule-based NER for the annotation of personal names, toponyms, organisations and time expressions (Ebling et al., 2011); improved lemmatisation for German separable prefix verbs and elliptical compound nouns (Volk et al., 2016); innovative techniques for sentence alignment in parallel texts (Sennrich and Volk, 2010); and the creation of a manually annotated parallel treebank with more than 1000 sentences in French and German for the purpose of assisting statistical machine translation (Göhring and Volk, 2011).

3 A Gazetteer-Based Approach to Geotagging a Heritage Corpus

Earlier work in geotagging our heritage corpus has relied largely on a gazetteer-based approach, targeting fine-grained geographic categories, such

Zur Bergnamenforschung.

(Noch einmal „rose", „ross".)

Von

Dr. C. Täuber (Sektionen Uto und Lägern).

Hätte nicht die Jahrbuchredaktion sich wiederholt über Mangel an Abhandlungen beklagt und ich nicht eine Menge von neuem Material und einige neue Gesichtspunkte zu den zwei früher publizierten [1]), kürzeren Artikeln über das Wort „rose" = Gletscher und „ross" in Verbindung mit Bergnamen beizufügen, so wäre ich auf dieses lehrreiche Thema nicht zurückgekommen. Es zeigt sich in weiten Kreisen der Bergfreunde ein so großes Interesse für die Deutung der oft rätselhaften Benennungen, und es ist auf dem Gebiete der Ortsnamen-Etymologie noch so viel zu arbeiten, daß wohl jeder neue Beitrag willkommen sein dürfte.

Den Ausgangspunkt meiner Forschungen bildete kein geringerer als der Monte Rosa, der Gletscherberg par excellence. — Es wird nun am richtigsten sein, daran anschließend eine Reihe von Gebirgslokalitäten mit ähnlich klingendem Stammwort, deren ich habhaft werden konnte, aufzuführen und hernach zu untersuchen, ob dieser Wortstamm überall der gleiche ist und den gleichen Sinn hat, endlich auch Belege aus andern Gebieten heranzuziehen.

1) *Monte Rosa*, höchster Grenzberg zwischen dem deutschen Wallis und Italien.

2) *Piano Rose*, ein Schnee- und Eisplateau südlich vom Theodulpaß, am Monte Rosa; auch *Piano Rosas* genannt.

[1]) Siehe „Alpina" 1906, pag. 89, und „Deutsche Alpenzeitung", 6. Jahrgang, Heft 7, pag. 171.

Figure 1: A page from the 1906 SAC yearbook with the article "On the research of mountain names".

as towns, mountains, lakes, glaciers, valleys and mountain cabins in order to enable location-based searching. Gazetteer-based approaches make use of curated lists of known geographic locations along with their relevant metadata (e.g. longitude and latitude, population, elevation, etc.).

Relying on gazetteers poses two major challenges. On the one hand, simple string matching with gazetteer entries can result in a high count of false positives due to the fact that toponyms often overlap with common nouns (e.g. Bath) and personal names (e.g. Washington). On the other hand, gazetteers are inherently incomplete and thus suffer from a lack of coverage, resulting in a high count of false negatives (Davari et al., 2019; Magge et al., 2018). However, gazetteers simplify the task of linking toponym mentions to their real-world referents. As such, they are typically unavoidable for automatically assigning geographic coordinates to a given toponym and have been a popular choice in geotagging historical and toponym-dense corpora (Won et al., 2018;

language	texts	tokens	token types	lemma types
German	12.8k	23.4m	769k	325k
French	12.8k	22.3m	418k	96k
Italian	0.16k	0.32m	39k	18k
Romansh	0.01k	0.014m	4k	0.2k
English	1.5k	6.5m	181k	60k

Table 1: Overview of our heritage corpus of alpine texts.

Moncla et al., 2014).

Our gazetteers were sourced from the Swiss Federal Office of Topography (SwissTopo)[3] and the community-based resource GeoNames[4]. We relied primarily on SwissTopo for identifying locations in Switzerland, while GeoNames was used to account for names of foreign mountain ranges and peaks that also frequently occur in the corpus.

Due to Switzerland's multilingual landscape, the same geographic entity often has different names in the local languages and dialects. For example, the *Matterhorn*, which straddles Switzerland and Italy, is also commonly referred to by its Italian name *Cervino* or the French name *Cervin*. In SwissTopo, however, names are listed only in the official language of the region, emphasising the lack of coverage associated with gazetteer-based approaches. As such, we have adopted numerous techniques to supplement our gazetteers.

Using the corpus itself as a resource, we extracted all words with suffixes typically denoting certain toponyms. For example, in German, mountain names often end with *-horn*, *-grat* and *-stock*. We then filtered out those mentions which are homographs of common nouns using a list collected from an online German dictionary[5]. The remaining unmatched words were then manually validated before being subsequently added to the gazetteer. Similarly, words which often serve as the first component of a multiword toponym in other languages, such as French *Cabane* and Italian *Rifugio* denoting cabins and French *Aiguille* and Romansh *Piz* for mountain peaks, were also leveraged to extract additional toponym candidates to extend gazetteer coverage. Furthermore, the most important exonyms (e.g. *Genfersee* for *Lac Léman*) and known spelling variants, such as hyphenated forms (e.g. *Monte-Rosa* for *Monte Rosa*) were also added.

Aside from additions, certain toponyms were also removed from the gazetteers in order to reduce the number of false positives. Since common nouns are capitalised in German, we deleted some toponyms which are homographs of frequent common nouns (e.g. *Nase* (nose)) as well as a handful of generic nouns denoting places (e.g. *Alptal* (alpine valley)).

Lastly, we extended toponym recognition beyond simple string matching to account for adjectives and prepositions that commonly occur in compound toponyms and can be inflected or even abbreviated (e.g. *gross* (big) in *Grosser Mythen*). Normalisation, lemmatization and decompounding were applied to address other inflections, such as genitive (*Bern* - *Berns*) and plural (*Fergenhorn* - *Fergenhörner*) forms (Volk et al., 2009).

3.1 Heuristics for Toponym Disambiguation

Despite the cautious crafting of gazetteers, not all ambiguities could be avoided. As such, we complemented our gazetteer-based approach with some simple heuristics to leverage internal contextual clues in an attempt to resolve both geo/non-geo and geo/geo ambiguities.

Geo/non-geo ambiguity occurs when a toponym has the same surface form as a non-toponym in the language (Amitay et al., 2004). For example, *Mönch* can refer to a mountain in Switzerland and the German word for 'monk'. A simple heuristic that helps to disambiguate between a toponym and a common noun is the occurrence of a preceding indefinite article. If the German article *ein* precedes *Mönch* in the same noun phrase, then it can only refer to the inhabitant of a monastery since it is not possible to use an indefinite article with a unique (i.e. definite) toponym in German.

[3] www.swisstopo.admin.ch

[4] www.geonames.org

[5] canoo.net

Geo/geo ambiguities arise when a single name has numerous real-world referents, for example, there are 17 different mountain peaks with the name *Schwarzhorn* in Switzerland alone. In general, an effective method for determining the correct referent of an ambiguous toponym is to use simple external heuristics based on prominence measures (e.g. population count) (Leidner and Lieberman, 2011), however, when dealing with fine-grained toponyms, such as mountain cabins or hiking trails (see Moncla et al., 2014), such measures are not suitable. In mountaineering and alpine texts, however, certain types of toponyms are often followed by their elevation (e.g. *Schwarzhorn, 3207 m*). Using this information, we resolved ambiguous toponyms by selecting the candidate from our gazetteer that has the closest elevation measurement. We restricted candidate selection to consider only the referents where the elevation does not deviate more than 50 metres from the measurement specified in the text. This prevents assigning the wrong geolocation given potentially erroneous information in the text. For those toponyms that could not be disambiguated with this approach, we assigned a placeholder referent ID. Toponyms listed in our gazetteer without a predefined ID from SwissTopo or Geonames received a 'null' ID. Table 2 displays the distribution of detected toponyms throughout the entire corpus. Here, linked IDs account for disambiguated toponyms while distinct types indicate the number of unique toponym IDs.

	total linked	total ambig.	total null	distinct types
cabin	20k	–	9k	0.3k
city	212k	20k	–	2k
glacier	15k	2k	10k	0.4k
lake	7k	0.7k	5k	0.3k
mountain	234k	72k	59k	8k
valley	28k	2k	19k	0.6k

Table 2: Corpus-wide toponym recognition and resolution ID counts for the gazetteer-based approach.

This gazetteer-based approach to toponym recognition, assisted by simple heuristics for toponym resolution, scores relatively high precision among most toponym types, yet suffers from low recall, particularly among frequent categories (see Table 4). Manual inspection reveals that prevalent historical spelling variations (e.g. *Fiesch* and pre-1905 *Viesch*) and the extensive use of endonyms for places in and around Switzerland (e.g. German: *Etsch* and Italian: *Adige*) remain a major challenge in identifying all toponyms in this corpus.

4 A Neural Approach to Geotagging a Heritage Corpus

In an attempt to improve upon the previous gazetteer-based approach, we adopt a neural approach to toponym recognition, inspired by current state-of-the-art techniques in NER. Similar to Huang et al. (2015); Ma and Hovy (2016), we apply a bidirectional recurrent neural network architecture (BiLSTMs) followed by a conditional random field (CRF) layer for the detection of toponyms in our corpus. This approach incorporates contextual string embeddings, as introduced by Akbik et al. (2018) in the Flair framework. Contextual string embeddings have been shown to perform well in downstream sequence-labelling tasks, such as NER. Due to the fact that they comprise character-level information, these embeddings are particularly well suited to modelling an open vocabulary.

We use a stacked embedding architecture (Akbik et al., 2018) to concatenate Flair's character-based forward embeddings trained on our corpus with general-purpose fastText word embeddings pre-trained on web data (Grave et al., 2018). The idea here is that the general-purpose embeddings provide sufficient global syntactic knowledge, while the in-domain Flair embeddings, which are trained on our own corpus, capture high-level contextual and orthographic idiosyncrasies typical for historical mountaineering reports.

4.1 Exploiting Gazetteer-based Labels as Silver Standard Training Data

Typically, the major challenge in machine learning and neural approaches to toponym recognition is acquiring domain-specific labelled training data (Davari et al., 2019). Therefore, we exploit the output of the gazetteer-based system described in Section 3, which acts as a low-effort silver standard and avoids having to rely on

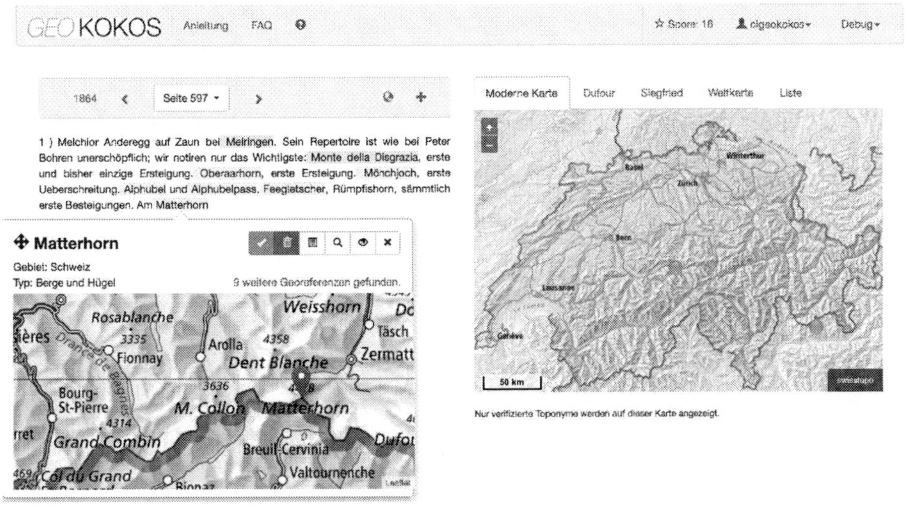

Figure 2: Screenshot of the GeoKokos citizen science web application.

time-consuming manual annotations. We extract sentences with at least one toponym from eight nineteenth-century yearbooks as the basis of our training data.

To increase the overall quality of the training material, we also integrate 1000 manually annotated sentences from two twentieth-century yearbooks. Finally, we extend the gazetteer-based annotations in the training set to cover toponym categories for rivers and regions, which had previously been ignored in our earlier approach, due to the fact that these entities are associated with multiple geographic coordinates.

The result of these steps is a hybrid 'silver-gold', toponym-dense training set consisting of approximately 15,000 sentences with more than 28,000 high-precision labelled toponyms. Using this initial training set, we establish a robust neural baseline model (see Table 4). For model tuning, we extract approximately 2,000 sentences, each with at least one toponym, from an additional yearbook as a silver development set.

4.2 Turning Silver to Gold with GeoKokos

In order to improve our neural model for toponym recognition, we aim to enhance the initial silver-gold training data by incorporating crowdsourced human annotations collected through the GeoKokos platform[6]. GeoKokos is a citizen science initiative designed to bring humans into the loop in order to resolve toponym recognition and resolution challenges that are problematic for fully automated techniques.

With GeoKokos we adopt a similar technique to Clematide et al. (2016), which made use of crowdsourced corrections for OCR errors. However, instead of relying entirely on human correction of the system output as done by Clematide et al. (2016), here, we iteratively collect new human annotations and use these to re-train our neural model. Then, updated model predictions are fed back into the system which, in turn, further assist users with their annotations.

GeoKokos provides an easy-to-use web interface (see Figure 2) that gives people the opportunity to select pages from certain yearbooks for reading and annotating. After registering an account, users have the option to delete, add, update and verify toponym annotations. Updating allows the user to alter the toponym category of an existing annotation, while interactive maps enable the user to verify and mark a toponym's location. For each correction action performed, users are awarded points. As noted by Clematide et al. (2016), even such a simple point-based statistic provides an aspect of gamification in linguistic annotations (Chamberlain et al., 2013) and, of course, friendly competition amongst users, which can be a strong motivator for those interested in the task or the content itself.

Through this process, an ever-growing number

[6] https://geokokos.ch

of crowd corrections will gradually turn our initial silver standard training set to gold, providing improved training data and hopefully resulting in ever better models for toponym recognition in our heritage alpine corpus.

4.3 Assisting Crowdsourced Toponym Resolution

For toponym resolution, we rely solely on the crowdsourced verification actions, which provide us with reliable geotagged annotations for those yearbooks available on GeoKokos. However, to assist users, we also incorporate a map-based approach (Buscaldi, 2011) for ranking potential geographic candidates. This algorithm assumes that textual proximity implies geographic proximity and consists of two main steps: candidate extraction and candidate ranking. First, we normalise all predicted toponyms in the text and extract a list of potential candidates from a database using string matches. Then, each candidate pair is scored and ranked according to their relative geographical proximity. Given all the toponym mentions on a single page, the geographically closest candidates receive the highest scores and are suggested to the user. This simple technique thus offers users a shortcut for verifying a toponym annotation, reducing the number of required clicks.

4.4 A Pilot Experiment with Crowd-Corrected Training Data

Since the ultimate goal of this approach is to iteratively learn and to benefit from the crowd-corrected annotations as early as possible, we conduct a pilot experiment based on a small amount of human annotations collected from the GeoKokos platform so far. Here, we expect the neural model to exhibit a high adaptive capacity in terms of recall, even when dealing with a small amount of crowdsourced annotations.

Table 3 displays the distribution of crowd correction actions performed on the two yearbooks chosen for this experiment. In total, we collected 831 corrections. Since our baseline training data consists of approximately 15,000 toponym-dense sentences sampled from the yearbooks available on GeoKokos, only 291 corrections were incorporated into the training data for this experiment.[7] Using these same sentences for training ensures comparability between the two models and allows us to assess the influence of these crowd-corrections.

action	1864	1874	total
untouched	2,467	4,185	**6,652**
others	39,317	57,826	**97,143**
verified	310	223	**533**
added	54	66	**120**
updated	45	79	**124**
deleted	35	19	**54**
total	**444**	**387**	**831**

Table 3: Crowd corrections for the SAC yearbooks from 1864 and 1874. 'Untouched' refers to silver standard toponym labels not changed by a user, while 'others' accounts for the remaining unlabelled tokens in these yearbooks.

5 Evaluation

Using a manually annotated gold standard of approximately 1,300 sentences created specifically for this task, we evaluate the two distinct approaches to toponym recognition in our heritage corpus of alpine texts. A direct comparison between the earlier gazetteer-based approach and our recent experiments in applying state-of-the-art neural models shows a promising increase in overall performance. Table 4 shows the evaluation scores per toponym label for the gazetteer-based approach, the neural baseline approach and our pilot experiment, which incorporates a small number of crowdsourced corrections.

The gazetteer-based approach shows strong performance for CABIN, LAKE and GLACIER, categories that are infrequent and tend to have rather regular and unambiguous suffixes in German (e.g. *-hütte* (cabin), *-see* (lake), *-gletscher* (glacier)). However, this approach suffers from low recall among more frequent categories where toponyms are generally more diverse. Comparing these results to the neural baseline, we see an increase in recall for the most frequent toponym categories MOUNTAIN (+6 p.p.) and CITY (+2 p.p.). This underlines the generalisation capacity of the neural approach to

[7] Since annotations are stored in IOB format, a correction implies that an O (outside) label was changed to a B (beginning) or I (inside) label via an addition action, or a B or I label was changed to an O label via a deletion action.

Category	Freq.	Gazetteer-based Prec	Gazetteer-based Rec	Gazetteer-based F_1	Neural Baseline Prec	Neural Baseline Rec	Neural Baseline F_1	Neural+annotations Prec	Neural+annotations Rec	Neural+annotations F_1
CABIN	3	1.0	1.0	1.0	0.50	0.34	0.40	0.75	1.0	0.86
CITY	89	0.74	0.61	0.67	0.78	0.63	0.70	0.77	0.68	0.72
GLACIER	20	0.95	0.80	0.87	0.95	0.80	0.87	0.95	0.85	0.90
LAKE	6	1.0	1.0	1.0	1.0	1.0	1.0	1.0	1.0	1.0
MOUNTAIN	225	0.92	0.62	0.74	0.93	0.68	0.79	0.88	0.75	0.81
REGION*	49	0.89	0.47	0.62	0.85	0.45	0.59	0.88	0.45	0.60
RIVER*	9	0.50	0.12	0.19	1.0	0.23	0.37	1.0	0.45	0.62
VALLEY	47	0.95	0.79	0.87	0.98	0.79	0.88	0.96	0.83	0.89
Micro average		**0.88**	**0.63**	**0.73**	**0.90**	**0.66**	**0.76**	**0.87**	**0.71**	**0.79**

Table 4: Precision, recall, and F_1-score for all toponym categories. *For the purpose of this evaluation, annotations for REGION and RIVER have been added to the original gazetteer-based approach using a gazetteer-lookup on the basis of normalised string matches.

toponym recognition in combination with context-sensitive string embeddings (Akbik et al., 2018) given sufficient training data.

Inspecting the results of our pilot experiment shows that the neural model is highly sensitive, even to a small number of integrated crowdsourced corrections. Taking into account the *n*-best predictions allows the model to output an alternative toponym label, which may not have received the highest probability, thus making it possible to flexibly increase the recall. Setting a probability threshold of 0.7 yielded the best results for this experiment. Here, we observe a noticeable improvement in recall across the board, resulting in a promising increase in the overall micro F_1-score on top of the neural baseline (+3 p.p.) and the gazetteer-based approach (+6 p.p.). These results indicate that a small amount of human-corrected annotations incorporated into the training set has a positive effect on the model's ability to identify new toponyms in the corpus. We expect that including more sentences containing crowd-corrected annotations in the training data will further improve the neural model.

6 Conclusion

In this paper we have presented two distinct approaches to geotagging a range of fine-grained toponyms in a heritage corpus of alpine texts. The goal of the earlier gazetteer-based approach was to achieve high precision for the purpose of reliable location-based searching. Consequently, this method also exhibited high counts of false negatives, resulting in low recall scores. This highlights the major shortcomings of relying on a finite list of known entities. Our new and ongoing approach relies largely on the previous work done in geotagging our corpus, while attempting to address the problem of low recall. Applying state-of-the-art contextual string embeddings and a neural model for toponym recognition allows us to attain a flexible system capable of predicting whether a given word constitutes a toponym based on the surrounding context, rather than relying solely on a list of previously known entities. Comparing these two approaches shows that the neural model outperforms the gazetteer-based system. Additionally, we have shown that the neural model responds well to even a small amount of crowd-corrected annotations. The GeoKokos platform enables us to efficiently bring humans into the loop to gradually turn our silver-standard training data to gold through an iterative learning process. As a result, it brings humans and machine learning techniques together, working hand-in-hand to improve geotagging in our heritage corpus.

References

Alan Akbik, Duncan Blythe, and Roland Vollgraf. 2018. Contextual String Embeddings for Sequence Labeling. In *Proceedings of the 27th International Conference on Computational Linguistics (COLING)*. Santa Fe, NM, USA, pages 1638–1649.

Einat Amitay, Nadav Har'El, Ron Sivan, and Aya Soffer. 2004. Web-a-Where: Geotagging Web Content. In *Proceedings of the 27th Annual International ACM SIGIR Conference on Research and Development in Information Retrieval*. Sheffield, UK, pages 273–280.

Davide Buscaldi. 2011. Approaches to disambiguating toponyms. *SIGSPATIAL Special* 3:16–19.

John Chamberlain, Karën Fort, Ugo Kruschwitz, Mathieu Lafourcade, and Massimo Poesio. 2013. Using Games to Create Language Resources: Successes and Limitations of the Approach. In Iryna Gurevych and Jungi Kim, editors, *Theory and Applications of Natural Language Processing*, Springer, page 42.

Simon Clematide, Lenz Furrer, and Martin Volk. 2016. Crowdsourcing an OCR Gold Standard for a German and French Heritage Corpus. In *Proceedings of the 10th Language Resources and Evaluation Conference (LREC)*. Portorož, Slovenia.

MohammadReza Davari, Leila Kosseim, and Tien D. Bui. 2019. Toponym Identification in Epidemiology Articles - A Deep Learning Approach. *arXiv preprint* arXiv:1904.11018.

Sarah Ebling, Rico Sennrich, David Klaper, and Martin Volk. 2011. Digging for Names in the Mountains: Combined Person Name Recognition and Reference Resolution for German Alpine Texts. In *Proceedings of the 5th Language & Technology Conference (LTC)*. Poznan, Poland.

Edouard Grave, Piotr Bojanowski, Prakhar Gupta, Armand Joulin, and Tomas Mikolov. 2018. Learning Word Vectors for 157 Languages. In *Proceedings of the 11th International Conference on Language Resources and Evaluation (LREC)*. Miyazaki, Japan.

Milan Gritta, Mohammad Taher Pilehvar, Nut Limsopatham, and Nigel Collier. 2018. What's Missing in Geographical Parsing? *Language Resources and Evaluation* 52(2):603–623.

Ann Göhring and Martin Volk. 2011. The Text+Berg Corpus: An Alpine French-German Parallel Resource. In *Proceedings of the 18th Traitement Automatique des Langues Naturelles Conference (TALN)*. Montpellier, France.

Zhiheng Huang, Wei Xu, and Kai Yu. 2015. Bidirectional LSTM-CRF Models for Sequence Tagging. *arXiv preprint* arXiv:1508.01991.

Jochen L. Leidner. 2007. *Toponym Resolution in Text: Annotation, Evaluation and Applications of Spatial Grounding of Place Names*. Ph.D. thesis, University of Edinburgh, Edinburgh, UK.

Jochen L. Leidner and Michael D. Lieberman. 2011. Detecting Geographical References in the Form of Place Names and Associated Spatial Natural Language. *SIGSPATIAL Special* 3(2):5–11.

Michael D. Lieberman, Hanan Samet, and Jagan Sankaranarayanan. 2010. Geotagging with Local Lexicons to Build Indexes for Textually-Specified Spatial Data. In *Proceedings of the 26th International Conference on Data Engineering (ICDE)*. pages 201–212.

Xuezhe Ma and Eduard Hovy. 2016. End-to-end Sequence Labeling via Bi-directional LSTM-CNNs-CRF. In *Proceedings of the 54th Annual Meeting of the Association for Computational Linguistics (Volume 1: Long Papers)*. Berlin, Germany, pages 1064–1074.

Arjun Magge, Davy Weissenbacher, Abeed Sarker, Matthew Scotch, and Graciela Gonzalez-Hernandez. 2018. Deep Neural Networks and Distant Supervision for Geographic Location Mention Extraction. *Bioinformatics* 34(13):i565–i573.

Ludovic Moncla, Walter Renteria-Agualimpia, Javier Nogueras-Iso, and Mauro Gaio. 2014. Geocoding for Texts with Fine-grain Toponyms: An Experiment on a Geoparsed Hiking Descriptions Corpus. In *Proceedings of the 22nd ACM SIGSPATIAL International Conference on Advances in Geographic Information Systems*. Dallas, Texas, pages 183–192.

Rico Sennrich and Martin Volk. 2010. MT-Based Sentence Alignment for OCR-Generated Parallel Texts. In *Proceedings of the 9th Conference of the Association for Machine Translation in the Americas (AMTA)*. Denver, Colorado.

Martin Volk, Noah Bubenhofer, Adrian Althaus, and Maya Bangerter. 2009. Classifying Named Entities in an Alpine Heritage Corpus. *Künstliche Intelligenz (KI) 4* pages 40–43.

Martin Volk, Simon Clematide, Johannes Graën, and Phillip Ströbel. 2016. Bi-Particle Adverbs, PoS-Tagging and the Recognition of German Separable Prefix Verbs. In *Proceedings of the 13th Conference on Natural Language Processing (KONVENS)*. Bochum, Germany.

Miguel Won, Patricia Murrieta-Flores, and Bruno Martins. 2018. Ensemble Named Entity Recognition (NER): Evaluating NER Tools in the Identification of Place Names in Historical Corpora. *Frontiers in Digital Humanities* 5:2.

Controlled Semi-automatic Annotation of Classical Ethiopic

Cristina Vertan
University of Hamburg, Germany
cristina.vertan@uni-hamburg.de

Abstract

Preservation of the cultural heritage by means of digital methods became extremely popular during last years. After intensive digitization campaigns the focus moves slowly from the genuine preservation (i.e digital archiving together with standard search mechanisms) to research-oriented usage of materials available electronically. This usage is intended to go far beyond simple reading of digitized materials; researchers should be able to gain new insigts in materials, discover new facts by means of tools relying on innovative algorithms.In this article we will describe the workflow necessary for the annotation of a dichronic corpus of classical Ethiopic, language of essential importance for the study of Early Christianity

1 Introduction

Although of major importance for the understanding of Christian Orient, the Gəʿəz language was up to now somehow neglected by the new research directions in Digital Humanities. Substantial material in digital form exist, but there are no tools which allow a deep analysis of the language and the content.

Improving our knowledge of the Gəʿəz language is crucial in order to refine our philological and text-critical methods as well as for advancing our understanding of thought and literature expressed in Gəʿəz.

This implies a substantial enlargement of the data by:

- seizing Classical Ethiopic texts in digital form
- adding significant linguistic information
- collecting metadata
- providing tools to interpret all this information.

The project TraCES[1] (From Translation to Creation: Changes in Ethiopic Style and Lexicon from Late Antiquity to the Middle Ages) aims to fill this gap by providing a collection of reliable and extensive linguistic data based on annotated of diachronic corpus of Gəʿz. The annotation and the developed tools will enable analysis at the level of lexicography, morphology and style. The annotated texts belong to different periods and genres of Ethiopic literature (text-critical editions). The project employs a multidisciplinary approach, involving methods from linguistics, philology and digital humanities. Major results expected to bring Gəʿəz in the digital era are:

- a (deep) annotated corpus linked with
- a lexicon (first digital lexicon for Gəʿəz)
- tools for the annotation, analysis, and visualization of the corpus, and browsing the lexicon.

In this paper we will focus on the description of the annotation tool. We will explain the requirements and the challenges these requirements imply for the tool development, and we will present its components, the underlying data structure as well as the linguistic -set.

2 Challenges of Gəʿəz language for digital tools

The digital annotation and analysis of any corpus, implies several steps:

- The identification of punctuation marks

[1] Funded thought the ERC Research Grant 2014-2019 (http// https://www.traces.uni-hamburg.de/about.html)

Proceedings of the Workshop on Language Technology for Digital Historical Archives in conjuction with RANLP-2019, pages 19–23,
Varna, Bulgaria, Sep 5, 2019.
http://doi.org/10.26615/978-954-452-059-5_004

- The identification of independent tokens (Tokenisation). By token we denote the smallest unit to which one can assign a part-of-speech (PoS).
- The division of the text in sentences.
- The construction of a linguistic tag-set (PoS + possibly attached features and their values)
- The annotation of these features as well as attaching to each word a lemma, and a link to a language lexicon

The Gəʿəz language belongs for the moment to the group of "very low resourced languages", i.e. languages which face a significant lack of resources (corpora , lexicons, terminological data bases, Thesemantic networks) and tools.(Maegard and Krauwer 2006) defines the minimum set of such resourced and tools which are necessary to insert one language on the digital map. Usually the problematic of (very) low resourced languages is solved through adaptation of existent material for other languages within the same family. In the case of Gəʿəz this is not possible due to several issues:

- Within the semitic language family the situation is better for Arabic and Hebrew. However classical variants of these languages are as well under-ressourced. The particularities of Gəʿəz writing system (alphabet, left-right writing) make impossible any adaptation
- From the point of view of the writing system Amharic seem to be the best next candidate for an adaptation. Amharic lacks itself language resources and tools. Additionally the morphological structure differs in many points from that one of Gəʿəz

There are a number of tools which claim to be language independent. These are tool developed with a statistical paradigm: very large language corpora are used and linguistic feature are learned from those. This paradigm cannot be followed for the moment for Gəʿəz as there exist no statistically relevant Corpus for classical Ethiopic Additionally machine learning methods are quite performant when the number of features to be learned is rather small. This is not the case of Gəʿəz, for which we identified over 30 0PoS

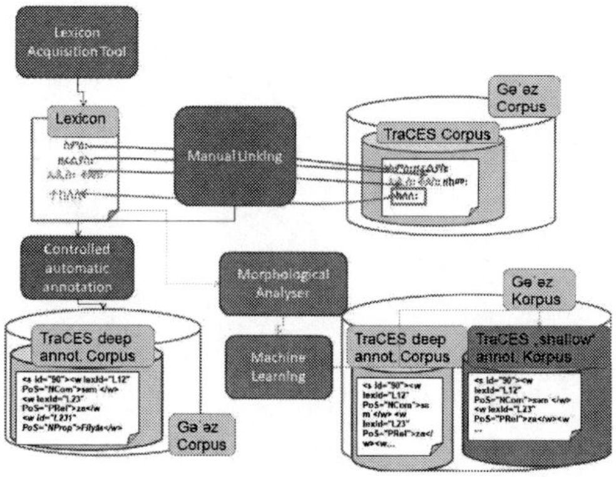

Figure 1 TraCES Modules for linguistic annotation

(Hummet and Druskat 2017) together with various features to be annotated.
An additional challenge is the absence of an electronic dictionary (lexicon) for Gəʿəz. Usually this is the first electronic resource to be developed for a language. Lexicons give important information about the lemma, the root as well as morphological features. The TraCES project builds the lexicon and the annotated corpus in parallel. This means that there is a bidirectional link between these 2 resources: already existing lemmas are marked in the lexicon but also new found words from the corpus are inserted (together with lemma and morphological information) into the lexicon.
A fully automatic annotation process is therefore for Gəʿəz impossible at this stage. We adopt a 2-stage workflow:

1. In a first stage a manual deep-annotated corpus is built. The manual Annotation is speeded-up by a controlled semi-automatic component, which will be explained in section 3
2. In a second stage the deep annotated corpus will be used as training material for a machine learning algorithm.

The complete architecture, including also the links to the lexicon component is presented in figure 1.

During last years several language-independent, respectively language customizable annotation tools were made available for researchers in humanities. Among those the most used are WebAnno (de Casthilo et. al 2014)) and CorrA (Bollmann et al. 20174) However a certain specificities of Gəʿəz made not possible the usage of these tools. In this section we will list these specificities and explain how they influenced the decisons taken for Annotation.

i) PoS Tagset

As mentioned the final goal of the TraCES project is to provide a framework which makes possible a diachronic analysis of this language. As usually variations in language occur at the micro and not the macro level, we need to perform a deep annotation which implies: a fine-grained PoS tag-set together with very precise and detailed features for each PoS. We defined a set of 30 PoS, grouped as follows:

- Nominals
  - Nouns: Common Noun, Proper Name
  - Pronouns: Independent Personal Pronoun, Pronominal Suffix, Subject Pronoun Base, Object Pronoun Base, Possesive Pronoun Base, Demonstrative Pronoun, Relative Pronoun, Interrogative Pronoun, Pronoun of Totality Base, Pronoun of Solitude Base
  - Numerals: Cardinal Numeral, Ordinal Numeral
  - Verb
  - Existentials: Existential Affirmative Base, Existential Negative Base
- Particle
  - Adverbs: Interrogative Adverb, Other Adverb
  - Preposition
  - Conjunction
  - Interjection
  - FurtherParticles: Accusative Particle, Affirmative Particle, Deictic Imperative Particle, Interrogative Particle, Negative Particle, Presentational Particle Base, Quotative Particle, Vocative Particle, Other Particle
- Foreign material
- Punctuation

The inclusion of different types of particles like Prepositions and Conjunctions or relative pronouns makes imperative a splitting of Gəʿəz word units in tokens e. g.
The word unit ዘፊልያስ፡ (*zafilyās*) will be split in ዘ፡(*za*) as relative pronoun and ፊልያስ፡ (*filyās*) as proper noun.
A more challenging issue is the annotation of pronominal suffixes which can be in fact marked just in the transliteration like in the following example:
The word unit በዓሡሩ፡ transliterated as *baʿāśuru* has the following tokens: *ba* (Preposition), *ʿāśur* (common noun) and *u (pronominal suffix)*. However the pronominal suffix u is part of transliteration of the Gəʿəz letter (ሩ). Thus an annotation of such part of part of speech can be done only on transliterations.
The linguistic annotation is just part of a more complex annotation as several layers (text structure, editorial marks, named entities like persons, places, date) some of them being more appealing if they are inserted in the original script.
The annotation tool must handle in parallel the text in its original form (fidäl) and transliteration

ii) Transliteration process

Given the motivation under i) we need for all texts their transliterated version. Time constraints make impossible a manual transliteration. On the other hand a fully automatic transliteration cannot handle (without apriori knowledge) phenomena like disambiguation of 6th grade (ə) or gemmination. There are no clear linguistic rules which could cover all cases. Moreover, even some rules my imply linguistic information, which at the moment of the transliteration is not available to the system. Unsupervised machine learning approaches (without training material) will not perform satisfactory as we do not have any big corpus in both fidäl and transliteration. Thus the annotation tool may support a kind of controlled semi-automatic transliteration 2 stages: first a rough transliteration, based on the general accepted transliteration rules is performed automatically. I-n a second stage corrections are done in a semi-automatic manner. We will explain this in section 4. The gemmination or disambiguation of 6th grade are linguistic motivated processes. From the technical point of view the linguistic annotation is preceeded by a tokenisation process (splitting or word units in tokens).

As consequence a gemmination (e.g.) may occur only after the PoS and its features are decided.

3 Underlying DataModel

The data model of the GeTa Tool follows an object-oriented approach. Each object can be located by a unique Id. There are two types of objects: Annotated Objects namely: Graphical Units, Tokens, Gəʿz-characters and Transcription-letters.

- Annotation Objects (spans) which are attached to one or more Annotation-Objects; these are: morphological annotations, text divisions, editorial annotations.

- Links between Annotated- and Annotation-Objects are ensured through the Ids. In this way the model enables also the annotation of discontinuous elements (e.g. a Named Entity which does not contain adjacent tokens).

- A Graphical Unit (GU) represents a sequence of Gəʿz-characters ending with the Gəʿz-separator (፡). The punctuation mark (።) is considered always a GU. Tokens are the smallest annotatable units with an own meaning, for which a lemma can be assigned. Token objects are composed of several Transcription-letter objects

e.g. The GU- Object ወይቤሎ፡ contains the 4 Gəʿz –letter objects ; ወ, ይ, ቤ, ሎ. Each of these objects contains the corresponding Transcription-letter objects, namely:

- ወ contains the Transcription-letter objects: *w* and *a*

- ይ contains the Transcription-letter objects: *y* and *ə*

- ቤ contains the Transcription-letter objects: *b* and *e*

- ሎ contains the Transcription-letter objects: *l* and *o*

Throughout the transliteration-tokenisation phase three Token-objects are built: *wa, yəbel,* and *o* Finally, the initial GU-Object will have attached two labels: ወይቤሎ and *wa-yəbel- o*. For synchronisation reasons we consider the word separator (፡) as property attached to the Gəʿz-character object ሎ.

Each Token-0bject records the Ids of Transcription-letter object which he contains.

Morphological annotation objects are attached to one Token-object. They consist of a tag (the PoS e.g. Common Noun) and a list of key-value pairs where the key is the name of the morphological feature (e.g. number). In this way the tool is robust to addition of new morphological features or PoS tags.

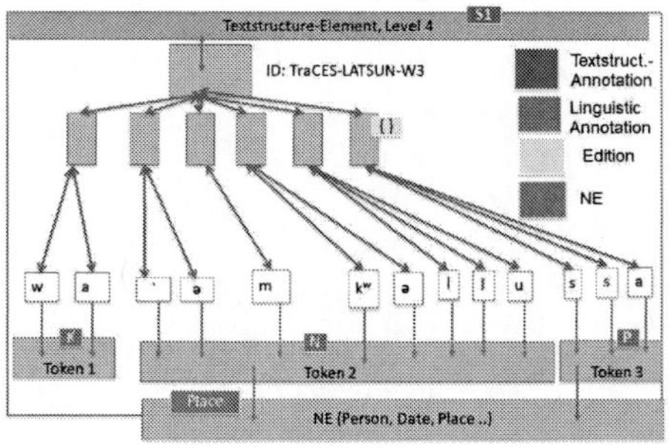

Figure 2 GeTa Data -model

As the correspondences between the Gəʿz-character and the transcriptions are unique, the system stores just the labels of the Transcription-letter objects. All other object labels (Token, Gəʿz-character and GU) are dynamically generated throughout a given correspondence table and the Ids. In this way the system uses less memory and it remains error prone during the transliteration process. In figure 3 we present the entire data model, including also the other possible annotation levels.

References

Bollmann, Marcel and Petran, Florian and Dipper,Stefanie and Krasselt, Julia 2014: *'CorA: A web-based annotation tool for historical and other nonstandard language data'*, in:Kalliopi Zervanou and Cristina Vertan and Antal van den Bosch and Caroline Sporleder (Eds.), Proceedings of the 8th Workshop on Language Technology for Cultural Heritage, Social Sciences, and Humanities (LaTeCH) Gothenburg, Sweden April 2014, 86-90.

Druskat, Stephan and Vertan, Cristina 2017, *'Nachnutzbarmachung von Forschungsdaten und Tools am Beispiel altäthiopischer Korpora'*, in

Gerog Vogeler (ed.) Kritik der Digitaler Vernunft Konferenzabstracts, Köln 2018, 270-273

Eckart de Castilho, Richard and Mújdricza-Maydt, Éva and Yiman, Seid Muhie and Hartmann,Silvana and Iryna and Frank, Anette and Biemann, Chris 2016, 'A Web-based Tool for the Integrated Annotation of Semantic and Syntactic Structures', in Erhard W. Hinrichs and Marie Hinrichs,and Thorsten Trippel (eds.), *Proceedings of the LT4DH workshop at COLING 2016*, Osaka, Japan: 76-84.

Hummel, Susanne and Wolfgang Dickhut 2016. 'A part of speech tag set for Ancient Ethiopic', in Alessandro Bausi and Eugenia Sokolinski, eds, *150 Years after Dillmann's Lexicon: Perspectives and Challenges of Gəʿəz Studies*, Supplement to Aethiopica, 5 (Wiesbaden: Harrassowitz Verlag, 2016), 17–29.

Krzyżanowska, Magdalena 2017. 'A Part-of-Speech Tagset for Morphosyntactic Tagging of Amharic', *Aethiopica*, 20 (2017), 210–235.

Maegaard, Bente and Krauwer, Steven and Choukri, Khalid and Jørgensen, Lars, 2006, 'The BLARK concept and BLARK for Arabic', in *Proceedings of the LREC Conference 2006*, http://lrec-conf.org/proceedings/lrec2006

Implementing an archival, multi-lingual and Semantic Web-compliant taxonomy by means of SKOS (Simple Knowledge Or-ganization System)

Francesco Gelati
Institut für Zeitgeschichte München — Berlin
Leibniz Institute for Contemporary History
Munich, Germany
gelati@ifz-muenchen.de

Abstract

This paper shows how a multilingual hierarchical thesaurus, or taxonomy, can be created and implemented in compliance with Semantic Web requirements by means of the data model SKOS (Simple Knowledge Organization System). It takes the EHRI (European Holocaust Research Infrastructure) portal as an example, and shows how open-source software like *SKOS Play!* can facilitate the task.

1 Introduction

Research projects, cultural heritage institutions, online repositories and catalogues often develop their own controlled vocabulary, which are primarily utilised as keywords in order to provide a thematic access to their entries. A catalogue entry that for instance displays "Refugee organisations" and "Relief and welfare organisations" in the metadata field "subjects" will be directly findable by users interested in these topics. This will be however possible so long as the users can browse the list of possible keywords, and perform keyword-based queries. In this paper I shall focus on a specific type of controlled vocabulary: taxonomies. Even though the term "taxonomy" is rarely used in human and social sciences, it is indeed the best option in order to describe hierarchical-structured controlled vocabulary, in the cultural heritage sector too. Cultural institutions are progressively sharing their catalogue entries, may they be archival descriptions, bibliographical records, museum data or digital objects, according to the FAIR principles. The same cannot unfortunately be said about their underlying taxonomies, which are simply not made exportable and reusable. Taking the EHRI (European Holocaust Research Infrastructure) Portal[1] as an example, I shall show in this paper how a taxonomy can be enriched with multilingual values and made interoperable by means of the semantic web data model SKOS[2] (Simple Knowledge Organization System) recommended by the W3C (World Wide Web Consortium), based on the RDF (Resource Description Framework) and compatible with the international standard ISO 25964-1 — Thesauri for Information Retrieval.

Some previous works: (Gelati, 2019), (Smith, 2018), (Vanden Daelen et al., 2015).

2 From Keywords to Taxonomies

The EHRI (European Holocaust Research Infrastructure) portal aims to aggregate digitally available archival descriptions concerning the Holocaust. This portal is actually a meta-catalogue, or an information aggregator, which imports datasets from a variety of data providers. Imported archival descriptions very often include the field "subjects" which bears keywords from the data provider's controlled vocabulary. Both archival descriptions and their keywords are written in many languages. In order to make keywords written in different languages equally findable, cross-lingual reconciliation is necessary. This concretely means that the English keyword "Refugee organisations" needs to be associated with its equivalent terms in all other supported languages (e.g. "organizacje uchodźców" in Polish). This is way EHRI developed a multilingual Holocaust and antisemitism-related taxonomy starting from previous hierarchies already used by partner institutions. The taxonomy was then made SKOS-compliant. Let us take a closer look to the SKOS specifications.

2.1 Concepts, Labels and Other Properties

"Concepts" are SKOS's main feature. Concepts

[1] `https://portal.ehri-project.eu/;forinfoontheprojectsee:https://ehri-project.eu/.`

[2] `https://www.w3.org/2004/02/skos/`

Proceedings of the Workshop on Language Technology for Digital Historical Archives in conjuction with RANLP-2019, pages 24–27,
Varna, Bulgaria, Sep 5, 2019.
http://doi.org/10.26615/978-954-452-059-5_005

"are identified with URIs, labeled with strings in one or more natural languages, documented with various types of note, semantically related to each other in [...] hierarchies and association networks, and aggregated into concept schemes".[3]

In our case, the EHRI taxonomy itself, called "EHRI terms"[4] is the concept scheme that incorporates all the concepts. Each term of the taxonomy (e.g. "Refugee organisations") is a concept, which is indeed provided with a URI, e.g.

```
https://portal.ehri-project.eu/
        keywords/ehri_terms-1199
```

and which can be expressed in all the natural languages[5] we wish by means of labels. Three types of label can be used: "preferred label", "alternative label" and "hidden label". In order to have a brief overview[6] of the rules, please note that, in order to avoid clashes, each concept may have no more than one preferred label for each language. The same value may not be used twice as preferred and as alternative value (nor twice as preferred and hidden, nor twice as alternative and hidden). Each concept may have as many preferred, alternative and hidden labels as wished. None of the three types of label is obligatory: a concept may have no labels at all, or may have for instance alternative label(s) only. Some of the above-mentioned concept "Refugee organisa-tions" preferred labels result as:

```
skos:prefLabel "Refugee
 or-ganisations"@en,
 "Flüchtlingsor-ganisation"@de,
 "organizacje uchodźców"@pl .
```

The fields "scope note", "definition" and "notation" may provide additional information or explanation on the concept.

```
skos:scopeNote "Refers both
 to refugees and to
 asylum-seekers
 organisations."@en .
```

[7]

The properties "narrower" and "broader" shape the hierarchical tree of the taxonomy. In our case, the concept "Refugee organisations" has two broader concepts, "refugees" and "organisations", whose URIs are expressed below.

```
skos:broader
    <https://portal.ehri-project.eu/
    keywords/ehri_terms-1196> ,
   <https://portal.ehri-project.eu/
    keywords/ehri_terms-304> .
```

The possibility to create associative (i.e., non hierarchical) links between two or more concepts is also provided by the property "related". Some more properties, the most important being the "class" option, are equally available.

2.2 Multilingualism

Multilingualism is a strong feature of the EHRI taxonomy, for the following languages are implemented: Czech, Dutch, English, French, German, Hebrew, Hungarian, Italian, Polish, Russian, Serbo-Croatian and Ukrainian. They encompass three scripts, i.e. Latin, Hebrew and Cyrillic. Hebrew is displayed in Hebrew characters only, Serbo-Croatian in Latin only, whereas Russian and Ukrainian are parallelly displayed both in Latin and in Cyrillic:

```
skos:altLabel "Організації
   допомоги біженцям"@uk ,
   "Organìzacìï dopomogi
   bìžencâm"@uk-Latn ;
skos:prefLabel "organizacii
   beženceV"@ru-Latn ,
   "организации беженцев"@ru .
```

The taxonomy can updated by uploading to the online catalogue a new version of the taxonomy as a SKOS-compliant turtle file (.ttl). It means that new or amended concepts and their labels can be introduced at any time. So can always new languages be implemented. A user-friendly and code-free option for managing an existing taxonomy, or creating a new one, would be the web-based open-source tool "SKOS Play!"[8].

2.3 Creating a New Taxonomy

SKOS Play! provides you with a sample Excel spreadsheet, where each column relates to a given

[3] https://www.w3.org/TR/skos-primer/

[4] https://portal.ehri-project.eu/vocabularies/ehri_terms/

[5] Hereafter will "language" or "natural language" always refer to the combination of a natural language and a script. It means that in this paper, simply for conciseness rather than for scientific purposes, Ukrainian written in Latin characters and Ukrainian in the Cyrillic script are considered two different languages.

[6] Please refer to https://www.w3.org/TR/2009/REC-skos-reference-20090818/ which is however at the moment of writing (2019-06-27) still a draft.

[7] Sample invented by the author.

[8] See: http://labs.sparna.fr/skos-play/. SKOS Play! is an open-source application developed by Thomas Francart for Sparna and released at the moment of writing under the licence CC-BY-SA 3.0.

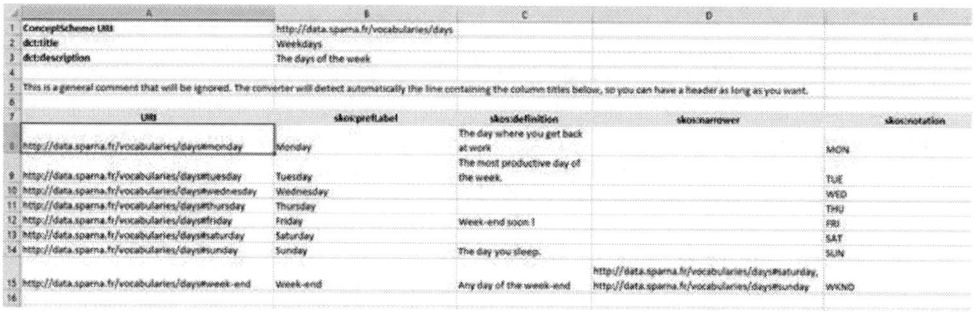

	A	B	C	D	E
1	ConceptScheme URI	http://data.sparna.fr/vocabularies/days			
2	dct:title	Weekdays			
3	dct:description	The days of the week			
4					
5	This is a general comment that will be ignored. The converter will detect automatically the line containing the column titles below, so you can have a header as long as you want.				
6					
7	URI	skos:prefLabel	skos:definition	skos:narrower	skos:notation
8	http://data.sparna.fr/vocabularies/days#monday	Monday	The day where you get back at work		MON
9	http://data.sparna.fr/vocabularies/days#tuesday	Tuesday	The most productive day of the week.		TUE
10	http://data.sparna.fr/vocabularies/days#wednesday	Wednesday			WED
11	http://data.sparna.fr/vocabularies/days#thursday	Thursday			THU
12	http://data.sparna.fr/vocabularies/days#friday	Friday	Week-end soon !		FRI
13	http://data.sparna.fr/vocabularies/days#saturday	Saturday			SAT
14	http://data.sparna.fr/vocabularies/days#sunday	Sunday	The day you sleep.		SUN
15	http://data.sparna.fr/vocabularies/days#week-end	Week-end	Any day of the week-end	http://data.sparna.fr/vocabularies/days#saturday, http://data.sparna.fr/vocabularies/days#sunday	WKND
16					

Figure 1: The *Skos Play!* Excel file sample.

property (e.g. preferred label), and each row to one single item (e.g. a concept).

You can download the spreadsheet and enter there your own values. Then you can upload it back to the tool and convert it from Excel to a Semantic-Web and SKOS-compliant turtle file (.ttl), which will look like:

```
@prefix skos:  <http://www.w3.org/
      2004/02/skos/core#> .
<https://portal.ehri-project.eu/
      keywords/ehri_terms-989/>
      a skos:Concept ;
skos:prefLabel "Fascist
        propaganda"@en.
<https://portal.ehri-project.eu/
      keywords/ehri_terms-342/>
      a skos:Concept ;
skos:prefLabel "Antisemitic
        propaganda"@en.
<https://portal.ehri-project.eu/
      keywords/ehri_terms-986/>
      a skos:Concept ;
skos:prefLabel "Propaganda"@en ;
skos:narrower
      <https://portal.ehri-project.eu/
         keywords/ehri_terms-342/> ;
skos:narrower
      <https://portal.ehri-project.eu/
        keywords/ehri_terms-989/>.
```

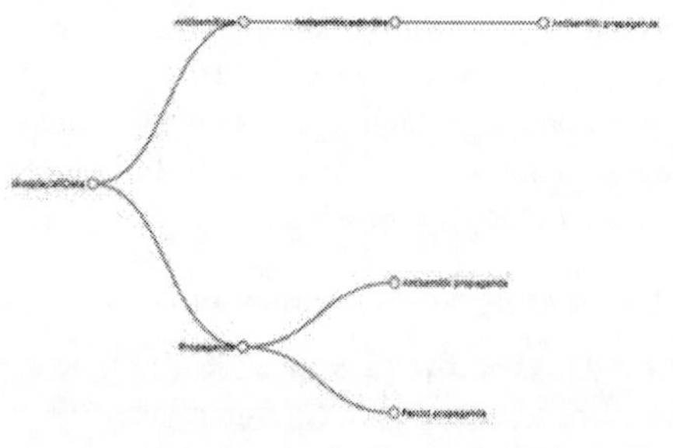

Figure 2: A *Skos Play!* visualisation option .

You may also visualise the data in a variety of options, amongst others as a tree.

2.4 Data Enrichment

Assigning URIs to all the entries of a digitally-shared taxonomy has many benefits. It permits first of all data enrichment from Linked Open Data multilingual databases like Wikidata.

One can automatically reconciliate identical entities, e.g. by means of the open-source programme Open-Refine.[9] One will then be able to associate the EHRI taxonomy entry "Propaganda" with its similar entry in Wikidata:

```
https://portal.ehri-project.eu/
      keywords/ehri_terms-986
=

https://www.wikidata.org/wiki/Q7281 .
```

It is also possible to manually create our own RDF triples, the standard way to make machine-readable affirmations. "Antisemitic propaganda is a category of Propaganda" may be expressed by means of the Wikidata property "subclass of"[10]: the former is a subclass of the latter will give

```
<https://portal.ehri-project.eu/
      keywords/ehri_terms-342/>
<https://www.wikidata.org/wiki/
      Property:P279>
<https://portal.ehri-project.eu/

      keywords/ehri_terms-986/> .
```

3 Conclusion

By means of the few steps described above, an online archival (meta)catalogue can make its multilingual taxonomy digitally available and machine-readable. The possibility to manage a SKOS taxonomy in a variety of formats (including TTL, RDF/XML and JSON), attribution of URIs (which the research body simply has to activate), linkage of information with leading open-source databases, compliancy with Semantic-Web

[9] http://openrefine.org/

[10] Whose URI is: https://www.wikidata.org/wiki/Property:P279

requirements... Everything makes the data FAIR: findable, accessible, interoperable and reusable.

Acknowledgments

The author, who was introduced by Ksenia Zaytseva and the Austrian Centre for Digital Humanities to SKOS, wishes to thank both of them, as well as the EHRI staff.

References

Francesco Gelati. 2019. Archival Metadata Import Strategies in EHRI. *ABB: Archives et Bibliothèques de Belgique - Archief- en Bibliotheekwezen in België*, Trust and Understanding: the value of metadata in a digitally joined-up world, ed. by R. Depoortere, T. Gheldof, D. Styven and J. Van Der Eycken(106):15–22.

Jeffrey Smith. 2018. Toward "Big Data" in Museum Provenance. In Giovanni Schiuma and Daniela Carlucci, editors, *Big Data in the Arts and Humanities. Theory and Practice*, pages 41–50. Taylor & Francis, Boca Raton, FL.

Veerle Vanden Daelen, Jennifer Edmond, Petra Links, Mike Priddy, Linda Reijnhoudt, Václav Tollar, and Annelies van Nispen. 2015. Sustainable Digital Publishing of Archival Catalogues of Twentieth-Century History Archives. In *"Open History: Sustainable digital publishing of archival catalogues of twentieth-century history archives"*, Brussels, Belgium.

EU 4 U: An educational platform for the cultural heritage of the EU

Maria Stambolieva
Centre for Computational and Applied Linguistics
New Bulgarian University
Sofia, Bulgaria
mstambolieva@nbu.bg

Abstract

The paper presents an ongoing project of the NBU Laboratory for Language Technology aiming to create a multilingual, CEFR-graded electronic didactic resource for online learning, centered on the history and cultural heritage of the EU (e-EULearn). The resource is developed within the e-Platform of the NBU Laboratory for Language Technology and re-uses the rich corpus of educational material created at the Laboratory for the needs of NBU program modules, distance and blended learning language courses and other projects. Focus being not just on foreign language tuition, but above all on people, places and events in the history and culture of the EU member states, the annotation modules of the e-Platform have been accordingly extended. Current and upcoming activities are directed at: 1/ enriching the English corpus of didactic materials on EU history and culture, 2/ translating the texts into (the) other official EU languages and aligning the translations with the English texts; 3/ developing new test modules. In the process of developing this resource, a database on key figures and imporant places, objects and events in the cultural history of the EU will be created. The target users of the resource are students aged 8-12. Along with creating a useful teaching resource for local students, the project also addresses problems facing migrant and minority learners, with the ambition to contribute to the social insertion of young learners in an age of increased people mobility. It has the support of the UN Refugee Agency (UNHCR).

1 Context

Whether young learners come to the EU from other parts of the world or move within the EU, they need to gain basic information about both their new country of residence and the European Union. Some of this information is taught or otherwise acquired by native children at a very early age, and is often taken for granted. Acquaintance with the rich and varied cultural history of Europe and the EU states can be an important factor for stimulating the desire of young learners to become part of this culture. The development of such thematic content in several EU languages, coupled with graded language tuition and translation, and via an open education multilingual e-platform, can offer substantial support to both students of foreign languages and cultures and to young learners accompanying their parents in transnational mobility.

Eurostat 2015 data indicate that as a result of intra-EU mobility and immigration from third countries, EU societies are becoming increasingly diverse. Roughly 10 per cent of the population of the European Union were not born in their country of residence; an increasingly large percentage of this population are children under 15. These "migrant children" have, as a rule, low educational performance and tend to leave school early. In spite of the considerable attention this problem has received in the past decades — from the Council of the EU 1977 Directive 77/486/EEC on the education of children of migrant workers to the more recent EC Green Paper "Migration and mobility: challenges and opportunities for EU educational systems", these children continue to suffer from "a negative penalty associated with migratory status".

The integration of migrant children is becoming a key problem for the successful development of the EU, for which — as analysts point out — solutions are yet to be sought, found and implemented. (Algan et al., 2010, p. 25) report that education systems do make efforts to integrate immigrant children, "though it is much harder to say whether progress is as fast as it could be". (Dumcius et al., 2013, p. 5) stress the necessity to adopt an integrated approach to the problem of child migrant

Proceedings of the Workshop on Language Technology for Digital Historical Archives in conjuction with RANLP-2019, pages 28–33,
Varna, Bulgaria, Sep 5, 2019.
http://doi.org/10.26615/978-954-452-059-5_006

inclusion, combining linguistic and academic support, parental and community involvement and intercultural education — an aspect also stressed by (Nusche, 2009) and (, ed.).

Driven by the seriousness of the problems outlined, our objective is the development of a multilingual EU History & Culture learner pack — e-EULearn — for young learners, with a common educational content, both language and content-based tests and quizzes, as an accessible introduction to EU cultures and languages. We identify the following subtasks:

- combining foreign language learning with a EU cultural context;
- creating a supportive environment for personalised and individualised online tuition, also suitable for refugee, migrant and minority children in the language of their new country of residence;
- offering methodological support to schools and teachers with up-to-date resources, tools and reference materials.

2 Online Education and the NBU e-Platform

An educational platform for the cultural heritage of the EU was initiated by the team of the NBU Applied Foreign Languages undergraduate program, where students from 16 countries study together, and of the NBU Language Technology Lab, which has recently worked on the generation of educational content for the language and cultural integration of migrant and ethnic minority children. The project stems from our experience in addressing problems that face migrant and minority learners and draws on positive results: a/ the success of courses developed and taught by our program team for a multicultural audience of undergraduate students, as e.g. *The Languages of the EU, EU Cultural History, Electronic Resources of the EU*, and others; b/ the success of distance learning language courses supported by an integrated platform for text annotation, semi-automatic extraction of training content and automatic assessment. The project builds on this know-how and on the accumulated corpus of texts on the history and culture of the EU to develop didactic content suitable for a target age group of students aged 8-12 and by extending the functionalities of the software support.

The e-EULearn pack for young learners is an educational resource presenting EU history and culture in graded CEFR texts and drills. The design of e-EULearn is based on the methodological principles of e-learning. Most often used as a supplement to traditional classroom tuition, e-learning is an invaluable means of increasing the overall effectiveness of the process of teaching — especially if sufficiently well planned and conceived as an integral part of this process. Effective distance or blended learning requires no less careful planning and preparation than traditional brick-and-mortar classes; and the simple addition of available online videos or tests to existing educational content might lend a course additional flavour but will not necessarily increase its effectiveness. While the needs of trainees are symmetrical, the groups are often heterogeneous. In designing the e-EULearn pack, we follow (McDonough and Shaw, 1993) who define a well-designed e-course as one that provides for personalisation and individualisation of the learning process. In line with (Hemingway, 1986) we will insist on providing students with the relative freedom to choose from a rich learning content, supplying them with the appropriate reference materials and with sufficient training tasks.

Online (distance, blended or self-directed) education is a learning option which, with the opportunities it creates for individualisation and personalisation of the educational process, is well suited to the needs of learners coming from different linguistic and cultural backgrounds and/or learners in need of additional tuition. An important condition for effective online learning is the availability of electronic resources and supporting software. NBU is among the leading HEIs in the region in the field of both e-education and language technology. Our accumulated know-how can now be put to the benefit of school education by directing efforts towards the development of tools and resources suited/adapted to the needs of our target learners.

3 The NBU e-Platform

The NBU e-Platform for Language Teaching and Research is a modular, versatile tool designed to provide 1/ course development support for native and foreign language (and literature) teachers and lecturers, 2/ data and tools for corpus-driven and corpus-based lexicography, corpus and contrastive linguistics, 3/ an environment for research, experimentation and comparison of new methods of language data preprocessing. It integrates: 1/ an environment for creating, organising and maintaining electronic text archives and extracting text corpora: a repository of domain-specific texts, further classified in accordance with the Common European Framework of Reference for Languages (CEFRL); 2/ modules for linguistic analysis, including a lemmatiser, an in-depth POS analyser; a term analyser; a syntactic analyser; an analyser of multiple word units (MWU — including complex terms, analytical forms, phraseological units); a parallel text aligner; a concordancer; 3/ a linguistic database allowing linguistic analysis to be performed on either a single text or a corpus of texts, with options for corpus manipulation (reduction in size or expanding with additional texts from the archive) without loss of information; 4/ modules for the generation and editing of vocabulary or grammar drills; 5/ modules for the extraction of linguistic information directly from texts/corpora or from the data base. The environment for the maintenance of the electronic text archive organises a variety of metadata which can, individually or in different combinations, form the basis for the extraction of text corpora. Following linguistic annotation, secondary ("virtual") corpora can be extracted. The platform with its data base can thus be used to support a variety of linguistic activities — from the generation of drills to the compilation of corpus-driven and corpus-based reference materials — glossaries, thesauri, dictionaries or grammars. The e-Platform can support all EU languages; of these, only three have been made active so far: English, French and Bulgarian.

The architecture of the system is modular and consists of input modules, modules for preprocessing, processing, analysis and data storage, and output modules. The input modules provide user interface for different linguistic tasks and work independently. The architecture allows for the addition of new modules, as well as various modules for automatic (pre)processing. Each of the preprocessing modules can be implemented independently and added to the system at an appropriate stage. The text-based drills generator can export the teaching content to the educational platform of the user. In the case of New Bulgarian University, the export format is Moodle XML format for Moodle Quiz Module. The e-platform feeds the question banks of Moodle with three types of question items: Fill in the Blanks, Matching, and Reordering, each with a number of subtypes. The architecture of the system is maintainable and extendable.[1]

For the purposes of this project, the NBU platform is being developed in several directions:

- its functionalities are extended to allow work with new languages: French, German, Spanish, Russian;
- the annotation tags are tailored to the new languages of the project;
- new annotation tags are added in answer to the focus on EU history and culture;
- new test options will be added to the test-generating functionality.

4 Virtual Corpora and the Re-use of Didactic Material

The "Virtual corpora" function of the e-Platform allows the extraction of token-based or annotation-based corpora from existing corpora and files. Figure 1 presents a list of subcopora, mostly generated from Wikipedia and tourist guides.

A virtual corpus can contain a word form (e.g. the 3rd person sg, pronoun *it*), a lemma, a part of speech (e.g. Numeral), the value of a grammatical category (e.g. Perfective Aspect — for Bulgarian or Russian). For the purpose of the EU 4 U project, the following new subcategories were introduced in the annotation module: Noun/Proper/Person, Noun/Proper/Place, Noun/Common/Hist&Cult (e.g. *tumulus* or *artefact*), Numeral/Cardinal (1885), Numeral/Ordinal (15th), Adjective/Proper (Byzantine), Adjective/Hist&Cult. This latter category contains adjectives identified as forming indicative contexts

[1] Cf.: Stambolieva et al. 2017a. M. Stambolieva, M. Hadjikoteva, M. Neykova, V. Ivanova, M. Raykova. 2017. The NBU E-Platform in Teaching Foreign Languages for Specific Purposes. Proceedings of the 13th Annual International Conference on Computer Science and Education in Computer Science, Albena. Stambolieva 2017b M. Stambolieva, M. Hadjikoteva, M. Neikova, V. Ivanova, M. Raikova. 2017. Language Technologies in Teaching Bulgarian at Primary and Secondary School Level: the NBU Platform for Language teaching. Proceedings of RANLP 2017 Workshop" LTDHCSEE: Language Technology for Digital Humanities in Central and (South-) Eastern Europe, 32-8. ISBN 978-954-452-046-5

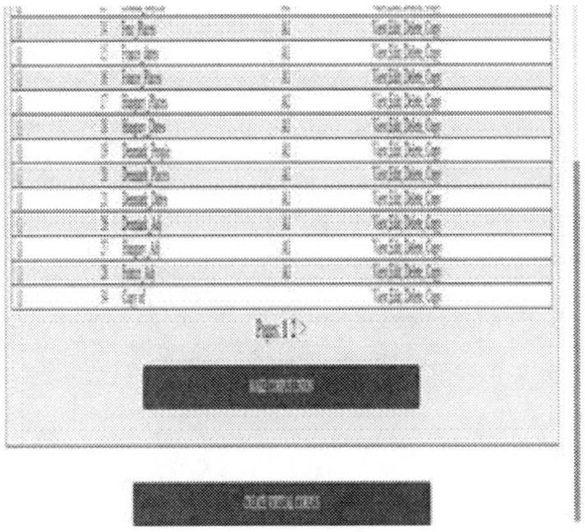

Figure 1: Virtual corpora.

for phrases referring to historical and cultural heritage. An indicative list of verbal contexts was similarly compiled.

Virtual corpora can, like other corpora in the platform, be manipulated: split or merged (united) with other corpora — Cf. Figure 2.

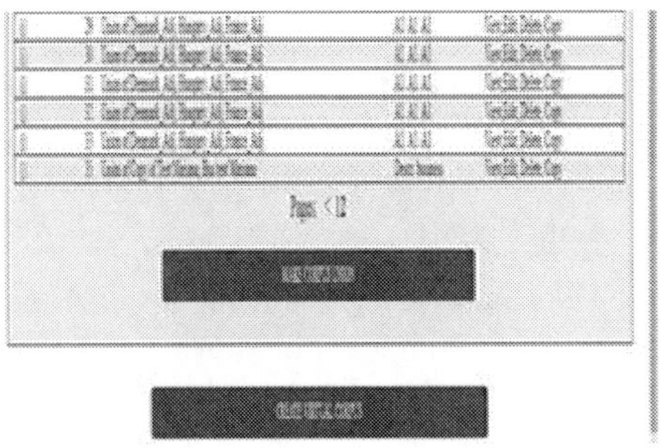

Figure 2: Union of corpora.

The unification of virtual corpora facilitates the generation of the didactic materials and tests focused on EU culture and history — by providing generalized lists of important people/places/events. Together with the text files and text-based corpora, they form the basis for the generation of our training materials — quizzes and tests.

5 Deriving EU History and Culture Tests from Virtual Corpora

The test generator of the e-Platform has two main modules: Matching, Fill in the Blanks and Reordering. Only the first two modules are actively used for this project. For them both, test generation starts by a choice of corpus, then of the test segments — relevant segments, or all segments (Select All) on which the test will be based — Cf. Figure 3.

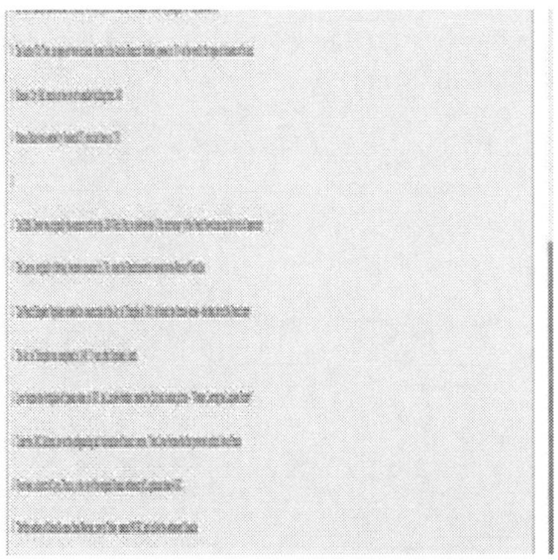

Figure 3: A CEFR A1 level corpus for four EU countries.

Texts and corpora, whether virtual or not, should be annotated (manually or otherwise) prior to test generation.

For the Fill in the Blanks module, tokens must be lemmatised and POS-tagged. The POS-tagger of the platform has been extended with the new subcategorisation values.

For the Matching module, the "definition" slot of the POS tagger can be used in a number of ways to link people to biographical notes, places and events, places to people and events, events to dates, people and places. The slot can also be filled with photographs and pictures of people and places.

When the selected segments are uploaded in the test generating module, the relevant tag must be chosen, the number of occurrences indicated (each, evey second, etc.), and the desired test type selected — multiple choice (in either drag-and-drop or dropdown format) or gapfill (open cloze). Once the test has been generated, the platform allows post-editing.

All texts entering the e-Platform are graded for CEFR levels A1-C2. For the purpose of this project, our corpora consist of short A1 and A2 level texts. Levels are defined with the help of Laurence Anthony's AntWordProfiler[2] but a more fine-grained and CEFR-level based profiler

[2] https://www.laurenceanthony.net/software/antwordprofiler/

of texts is planned as a project-related task. Another task yet to be defined and implemented is the manner of integration of the aligned bilingual texts into the EULearn lesson pack, the types of reference and training resources that can be derived from them.

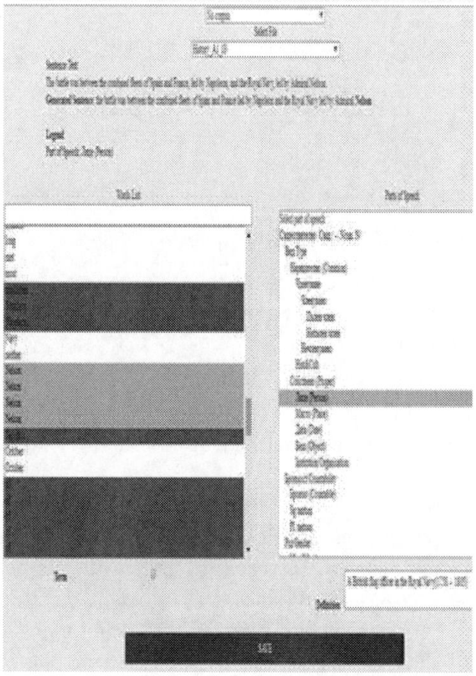

Figure 4: Annotation.

Texts and training materials will be carefully sequenced in Moodle lessons to facilitate step-by-step learning: students will first be asked to link people and events to centuries, then do multiple choice training tests, followed by open cloze ones. They will learn to link names and places with photographs, pictures or short texts, to link people, places and events with countries. The Moodle educational platform where the training exercises are exported also allows the addition of audio/video tips to the tests and quizzes, and learning there can be fun. To ensure personalization, a considerable choice of didactic materials and audiovisual aids as well as a choice of languages will be offered. The possibility for self-paced learning in the flexible Moodle lesson structure offers individualization of the learning process.

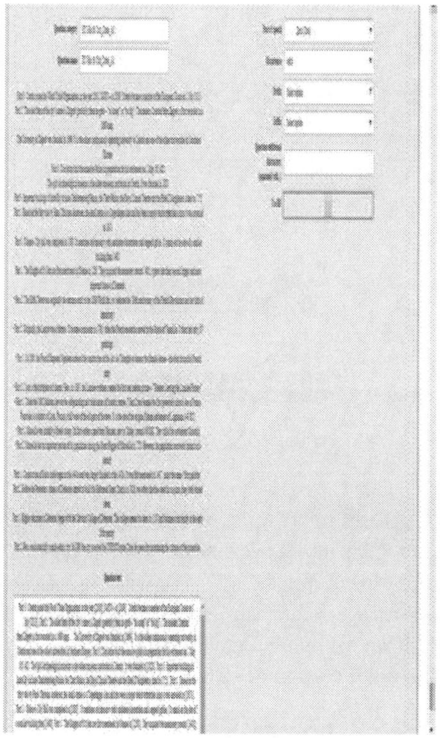

Figure 5: Generating a test on the history and culture of the EU.

6 Conclusion

The texts, data base and training materials developed within the project will form a useful resource with data related to people, places, objects and events in the cultural history of the EU, and links between them. While initially planned to provide learning support for children migrating across borders, the EULearn pack can offer useful additional materials for native children learning a foreign language and culture or for other educational purposes. The data base and the aligned texts can offer support for translation studies and linguistic research.

References

Yann Algan, Christian Dustmann, Albrecht Glitz, and Alan Manning. 2010. The economic situation of first and second-generation immigrants in france, germany and the united kingdom. *The Economic Journal*, 120(542):F4–F30.

Rimantas Dumcius, Hanna Siarova, Jana Huttova Ides Nicaise, and Indre Balcaite. 2013. Study on educational support for newly arrived migrant children.

Julia Szalai (ed.). 2011. Contested issues of social inclusion through education in multiethnic communities across europe. *EDUMIGROM Final Studies*.

P. Hemingway. 1986. Teaching a mixed-level class. In *Practical English Teaching*, pages 18–20.

J. McDonough and C. Shaw. 1993. *Materials and Methods in ELT*. Blackwell, Cambridge, Mass.

Deborah Nusche. 2009. What works in migrant education? *A Review of Evidence and Policy Options.' OECD Education Working Papers*, (22).

Modelling linguistic vagueness and uncertainty in historical texts

Cristina Vertan, Walther v. Hahn
University of Hamburg Department of Computer Science, Research Group"Computerphilologie", Vogt-Kölln Strasse 30, 22527 Hamburg, Germany
cristina.vertan@uni-hamburg.de,
vhahn@informatik.uni-hamburg.de

Abstract

Many applications in Digital Humanities (DH) rely on annotations of the raw material. These annotations (inferred automatically or done manually) assume that labelled facts are either true or false, thus all inferences started on such annotations us boolean logic. This contradicts hermeneutic principles used by humanites in which most part of the knowledge has a degree of truth which varies depending on the experience and the world knowledge of the interpreter. In this paper we will show how uncertainty and vagueness, two main features of any historical text can be encoded in annotations and thus be considered by DH applications.

1 Introductions

Most Digital Humanities projects tend to collect data as facts in a (relational) data base. According to Wilhelm Dilthey humanities make use of a hermeneutic paradigm for establishing hypotheses. Accordingly, social data often consist either of texts mirroring attitudes, allegations, beliefs, etc., or are reactions of test subjects to verbal stimuli. Such material cannot reasonably be treated as facts like numbers or positive propositions. On the other hand, analysing only formal features in the material does rarely contribute to the hermeneutic aims of the investigation intended by a humanist researcher. In this paper we show by means of a particular historical corpus how vagueness and uncertain language features can be kept in annotations and used in reasoning engines.

1.1 Case study: The corpus of historical texts wriiten by Dimitrie Cantemir

Dimitrie Cantemir (1673-1623) was prince of Moldavia (historical region including regions from current eastern part of Romania, Republic of Moldavia and some parts from Ukraine), man of letters-philosopher, historian, musicologist, linguist, ethnographer and geographer. He received education in classical studies (Greek and Latin in his country of origin), then he lived for several years in Istanbul where he learned Turkish, and familiarized himself with the cultural traditions of the ottomans, meet important persons around the sultan and learned a lot about history of the Empire. After a very short period of being prince of Moldavia he was forced to immigrate to Russia, where he became an important person at the court of Tsar Peter the Great. During this period, his works gained attention in the Western countries. He became member of the Royal Academy in Berlin and, at their request, he produced the two books which are the subject of this project:

Descriptio antiqui et hodierni status Moldaviae, written in Latin, a history of his country in which he describes not only pure historical facts but also traditions, the language, the political and administration system. Local denominations and troponins, as well as names are written in Romanian with Latin script as his intention is to demonstrate the Latin origin of his folk. The transcriptions are not standardized and one retrieves for the same troponin several name variations. Quotations as known today are very rare, there is no bibliography. According to (Lemny 2010), as there was practically no consistent previous work about the region, Cantemir himself was not particularly careful with indicating sources of knowledge. The work is accompanied by a map, the first detailed cartography of the region. The names on the map are in Romanian language. The Latin original was translated for the first time in German, and only later at the middle of the XIXth century in Romanian. The Latin manuscript seemed to be lost for a long time, so that the first Romanian translation was following the German one. The German translation is containing editorial notes of the translator

Proceedings of the Workshop on Language Technology for Digital Historical Archives in conjuction with RANLP-2019, pages 34–38,
Varna, Bulgaria, Sep 5, 2019.
http://doi.org/10.26615/978-954-452-059-5_007

(Cantemir 1771).The first parallel Latin-Romanian Edition considering all available manuscripts was publisher recently (Costa 2015).

Historia incrementorum atque decrementorum Aulae Othomanicae, the history of the Ottoman Empire. In contrast with the previous work about Moldavia, here Cantemir indicates very carefully the sources of information. (Lemny 2010) supposes the existence of previous works, known in the western countries, behind this decision. This work was written also at the request of the Academy in Berlin. Cantemir follows the same principle: text in Latin, while the troponins and local denominations are written this time in Ottoman Turkish. Although there were already some previous works about the Ottoman Empire, the novelty of his approach is the quotation of Turkish sources. The reliability of these sources is untrusted sometimes by Cantemir himself. The manuscript reaches the western world after Cantemir's death, carried by his son to London. Here, a first translation in English is produced: The history of Raise and Decay of the Ottoman Empire. The translator reinterprets the texts, probably also being confused by the presence of Turkish information sources, which were perceived in that time as completely unreliable. The Latin original remains lost for centuries and is rediscovered only at the end of the XXth century in the USA. Thus, the German translation (Cantemir 1745) is based on the English one and inherits the same alterations, and presumably adds new ones. The Romanian translations use in contrast the Latin original. The last translation (Costa 2015) will be used in this proposal.
Until now there is no systematic study on the reliability of the text sources in Cantemir's works, nor the degree of alterations produced by the translations of the two works.
Given the fact that both works became standard reference for western authors until the middle of XIXth century, it is expected that their reception influenced also following historical material. There is no reprint / new edition of his works in German or English. There are however, several reprints of the Romanian versions. Recent Romanian translations of Decriptio Moldaviae are done after the original Latin manuscript.
A lot of works were dedicated to the personality of Dimitrie Cantemir and its perception in different parts of Europe. A study of the reliability and consistency of the historical facts as they are described in originals and their translations is practically impossible to be done only with traditional hermeneutic methods. One needs expertise in the same time in Latin, German, English, Romanian, Turkish, just to enumerate the main languages used in the two books, which additionally sum up to a volume of about 1000 pages. Both German editions are printed in "Fraktur" script, which is nowadays very difficult to be read. A recent digitalization done by the BBAW for the History of the Ottoman Empire, makes the text more accessible. The digital version is freely available in TEi-P5 format. However, the TEI-P5 concentrates only on a diplomatic transcription and a flat linguistic annotation (lemma and part of speech) and does not touch any aspects of vagueness or reliability of sources.
Cantemir's texts are a real challenge with respect to multilinguality: in Descriptio Moldaviae, the original version in Latin there are paragraphs classical Greek, Romanian and isolated in Turk ish. The Romanian Names are written with Latin characters, unusual for that period (Romanian was written until the middle of XIXth century with Cyrillic script). Thus, the transcriptions in Latin script is random because Cantemir uses sometimes the rules used at the Moldavian court, and some other times, the Polish system to translate Cyrillic (Nicolae 2004). The German translation imports original Romanian names for troponins, persons or professions, and tries to adapt it to the German Phonetics which increases once more the variants for one single name.
Given the:

- Geographic distribution of material (originals in libraries in USA and Russia; translations and copies across Europe; most part of the quoted sources in Turkey),
- The multilingual character of the materials to be investigated (Latin, German, Romanian, English, Turkish at least) and
- The volume of data which has to be processed in parallel

no study about the reliability and consistency of the original and the translations could be performed until now.

In the HerCoRe project we propose the mix hermeneutic and IT-methods in order to:

- compare the copy of the original (Latin) and the English and German translations

- identify translations mistakes or gaps (done by purpose or not);
- search after the quoted works and identification of related ottoman sources;
- analyse Cantemir's writing and discourse style;
- asses the importance of the work in the ottoman studies and compare them with other works contemporary with Cantemir or follow-up research about the ottomans;
- develop electronic resourced which may be of use for follow-up works about the ottoman empire and the history of Balkans.

For these purposes we combine methods from natural language processing, ontology reasoning and fuzzy modelling which we describe in the following sections

2 Annotation of Vagueness

For the particular corpus presented in section 1.1 we decided to represent vagueness and other types of uncertainty at least five levels (Vertan et al 2017)

1. the text uncertainty (uncertain readings, losses, translations, multilinguality, etc.),
2. the linguistic vagueness (metonymies, vague adjectives, comparatives, non-intersectives, hedges, homonyms,),
3. the author reliability (genres, time style, general recognition),
4. the factual uncertainty (range expressions, time expressions, geo relations), and
5. historical change (named entities, abbreviations, meaning changes).

In a first phase we collect for each of the processed languages (German, Romanian and Latin) explicit lexical vagueness markers like words or expressions such as:

- Vague quanitfiers, e.g.: some, most of, a few, about, etc.
- Modal adverbs, e.g.: probably, possibly, etc.
- Verbs e.g.: to believe, think, prefer, etc.
- Lexical quotation markers, e.g. introduced by quotation marks or verbs with explicit meaning (say, write, mention)
- Inexact measures and cardinals
- Complex quantifiers
- Non-intersective adjectives
- Implicit syntactic clues: mainly verb moods such as conditional-optative for Romanian, conjunctive mood or imperfect/pluperfect for Latin, all of them indicating a non-reality (doubt, hear-say, possibility, etc.)

To annotate vague expressions like the ones above, the first step is to (semi-automatically) identify them. Identifying the three distinct categories of expressions that induce vagueness (explicit-lexical, implicit-syntactic and pragmatic) requires different strategies.

To automatically identify (mark up in text) the explicit lexical-semantic clues, our strategy is the following: one manually create a list of words and expressions that are possible indicators of vagueness for the three languages (Latin, Romanian and German), from selected parts of texts. After the pre-processing step (chunking, lemmatizing, PoS tagging, NP-chunking), based on the previously created list, one automatically finds and marks all the (inflected forms of) explicit vagueness terms. Finally, one manually checks the marking for a short part of text for evaluation, followed by feedback and slight improvement.

The automatic identification of syntactic clues is a much more difficult/complex task. There is an inherent ambiguity in the text between vagueness and plain quotation (often intentionally created by the author) that is difficult to decide upon even for a human annotator, and thus impossible for the machine. A possible strategy to be investigated is: to use machine learning techniques (may be the power of deep learning) on a training set of positive examples obtained from explicit clues and negative examples of certain text.

Uncertainty is especially given by named entities like persons and places, especially when they differ in transliteration, spelling within the text or across similar historical sources. Thus the annotation of named entities is of central role.

However, the unclear person, time, place identification is even more difficult to automatize or at least assist by computer techniques, being more of a matter of hermeneutical research for humanists and historians.

The annotated entities are modelled as individuals within a knowledge-base which we will describe in the following section.

3 Fuzzy ontological knowledge base

The knowledge base of the system is ensured by a manual developed ontology written in OWL 2 (Bobillo et al 2010)), modelling the administrative, religious, military and conceptual world of the Ottoman Empire and the Moldavia and Wallachia Principalities. The ontology is built according to the current generally accepted sate-of the art concerning the history of this territories. In this section we will detail on three main features of the ontology

The modelling of time: As for may events and biographical data only uncertain dates are available we decided to represent a year not as a string , reflected then in other concepts as a Datatype Property but as an object (thus a concept into the ontology). Each concrete year is thus an instantiation of this concept. For a "*Year*"-concept we specify the

- *exactValue* a string
- *aroundValue, beforeValue, afterValue,* defined as fuzzyDatatypes
- *shortBefore, shortAfter* values defined as a combination between a modifier and a fuzzy datatype

The modelling of geographical regions: there are a number of geographical places for which the concrete placement is still not clear. For this we define a concept *GeographicalVagueZone* having as properties fuzzy datatype *neighborhoodOf*

The modelling of historical political entities: We distinguish between fixed concepts and relations (like geographical elements: river, mountain, island) and notions for which several "contexts can be defined. E.g. a geographical notion like "Danube" is within one historical context a border of the administrative notion "Ottoman empire", and in another one the border to the so called administrative notion "Roman empire". The historical contexts are specified by further objects containing fuzzy data properties (e.g. time, placement).

3.1 Conclusions and further work

Annotation and interpretation of vagueness is a central issue in digital processing of historical texts. However, this issue was completely neglected until now, and has as consequence often distorted interpretation of digitized historical texts. In this article we presented the current state of the art on vagueness annotation and introduce the first approached for considering vague expressions as part of the annotation process. We describe also the introduction of fuzzy properties into the ontological knowledge base as main backbone for interpretation of vague and uncertain facts Further work concerns the completion of the ontology, the linkage between the ontology and the corpus and the adaptation of a fuzzy reasoner (as in Bobillo et al 2013) dealing with the different types of annotations

Acknowledgements

Research described in this article is supported by HerCoRe project, funded by Volkswagen Foundation (Project no. 91970)

References

Bobillo, Fernando and Straccia, Umberto, 2010, "*Fuzzy Ontology Representation using OWL 2*", http://arxiv.org/pdf/1009.3391.pdf (last retrieved 28.08.2019)

Fernando Bobillo and Delgado, Miguel and Gomez-Romero, Juan, 2013, *Reasoning in Fuzzy OWL 2 with DeLorean, in Uncertainity Reasoning for the Semantic Web II,* in Bobillo, F.,Costa, P.C.G.,dAmato, C.,Fanizzi, N.,Laskey, K.B.,Laskey, K.J.,Lukasiewicz, Th.,Nickles, M.,Pool, M. (Eds.), Lecture Notes in Artificial Intelligence, Springer Verlag

Ioana Costa 2015, *Dimitrie Cantemir, Istoria măririi şi decăderii Curţii othmane,* 2 volume, editarea textului latinesc şi aparatul critic Octavian Gordon, Florentina Nicolae, Monica Vasileanu, traducere din limba latină Ioana Costa, cuvânt înainte Eugen Simion, studiu introductiv Ştefan Lemny, Bucureşti, Academia Română-Fundaţia Naţională pentru Ştiinţă şi Artă, 2015. ISBN 978-606-555-135-0 (978-606-555-136-7, 978-606-555-137-4)

Wilhelm Dilthey,1922, *Einleitung in die Geisteswissenschaft.* .

Cantemir, Dimitrie, 1771, *Beschreibung der Moldau, Faksimiledruck der Originalausgabe von 1771*, Frankfurt und Leipzig

Cantemir, Dimitrie, 1745 *Geschichte des osmanischen Reichs nach seinem Anwachse und Abnehmen*, 1745, Herold, Hamburg

Stefan Lemny, Stefan, 2010, Cantemirestii -A*ventura europeana a unei familii princiare din secolul al XVIII-lea*, Polirom Publishing House.

Nicolae, Florentina, 2004, *Toponime si Hidronime in literature Cantemiriana*, Annals of Philology XV, pag., 143-152

Cristina Vertan and Anca Dinu and Walther v. Hahn, 2017, On the annotation of vague expressions: a case study on Romanian historical texts, Proceedings of the RANLP 2017 Workshop on Language Technology for Digital Humanites in Central and South Eastern Europe

Author Index

Association for Computational Linguistics
209 N. Eighth Street
Stroudsburg, Pennsylvania 18360

ISBN 978-1-7138-0298-3

9 781713 802983

CURRAN ASSOCIATES INC.
proceedings.com

8th Workshop on Patent and Scientific Literature Translation 2019

Held at Machine Translation Summit XVII

Dublin, Ireland
20 August 2019